Praise for *Calm, Cool, and Connected*

Calm, Cool, and Connected is the book I have been wishing someone would write. Filled with practical insights and helpful tips, it is a manifesto for all of us parents who are navigating the new frontier of raising kids who have the world at their fingertips, literally. If you ever struggle with guilt about how much your kids are on screens or wage battle with your own proclivity to check email six times an hour, Arlene offers sanity without shaming and provides a way forward that is both life giving and realistic.

MANDY ARIOTO
President and CEO of MOPS International and author of *Starry-Eyed: Seeing Grace in the Unfolding Constellation of Life and Motherhood*

In this screen age of distraction, disconnection, and addiction, *Calm, Cool, and Connected* offers us a better way. Thank you Arlene—this book is timely, extremely practical, and a great resource.

SYLVIA HART FREJD
Founder and Executive Director, Center for Digital Wellness, Liberty University

Would you like a healthier family life? More joy? Deeper connections? Have you noticed your children being stressed and anxious? What about you? Arlene Pellicane will help you see how your technology use is relevant. Yes, yours. Children tell me all the time that they wish their moms would put down their phones. Many moms want to. Arlene will help you do that and more. Her personal illustrations, compelling data, and practical ideas will inspire you to make realistic changes. They're doable, directly related to real concerns, and will result in greater contentment. You can lear~ ~~ ~~ ~ ~~w and better you!

KATHY KOCH
Founder/president of Cel
of *Screens and Teens: Cor*
Wireless World

In today's culture, no longer are phones used just for calling; instead, they are multipurpose mechanisms that are calling the shots in our lives—dictating how we spend a great majority of our daily waking moments. As a result, I can only think of about three people I know personally—who don't own a cell phone—that wouldn't benefit from the advice in *Calm, Cool, and Connected*. For the rest of us, the time is long overdue! Arlene's wise insight into this tangled, technical problem coupled with scads of creative, concrete solutions will inspire you to put down your devices so you can spend less time touching screens and more time touching lives instead.

KAREN EHMAN
Proverbs 31 Ministries speaker and *New York Times* bestselling author of *Keep It Shut* and *Listen, Love, Repeat*

Arlene Pellicane has addressed head-on the silent foe of our day—our dependence on technology. As we steward ourselves and the next generation, all moms should read *Calm, Cool, and Connected*! It's a beautiful blend of practical and spiritual reasons why our dependence on cellphones harms the very things we long for most. Arlene wraps the warnings about the hidden dangers of our phone in a way that brings hope and reminds us, it's not too late to change.

GLYNNIS WHITWER
Author of *Doing Busy Better*
Executive Director of Communications at
Proverbs 31 Ministries

Arlene's words convicted me from the moment I saw the title! The sentence that spoke the most to me? "Your spouse is more interesting than your phone." This book gave me the reasoning and motivation to back away from my screen and take steps toward those I love.

DANNAH GRESH
Creator of Secret Keeper Girl and author of *The 20 Hardest Questions Every Mom Faces: Praying Your Way to Realistic, Biblical Answers*

Calm, Cool, and Connected is not only a great guidebook to creating intentional relationships and healthy living but it also provides suggestions for how to live life more fully face-to-face. Our lives are fuller because we choose to connect with others in real time and limit greatly the screen time in our home. Kudos to Arlene for addressing a growing problem in our society in a very practical and useful way.

JOANNE AND DAN MILLER
Authors, *Creating a Haven of Peace* and
48 Days to the Work You Love

In this excellent and timely book, author Arlene Pellicane has defined a plan for staying connected in this electronic age. Through building a productive, yet cautious relationship with one's devices, you can be calm, cool, and connected.

MEL CHEATHAM
Clinical Professor of Neurosurgery

If you sometimes struggle, as I do, to use technology in a balanced way, *Calm, Cool, and Connected* is a must read. Arlene offers practical suggestions and doable strategies that will equip you to be more intentional when it comes to your screen time.

ASHLEIGH SLATER
Author of *Braving Sorrow Together* and *Team Us*

It is a two-edged sword, this digital age. Like dynamite, digital tools can be a force for greatness in connecting people and creating opportunities; however, on the other hand, digital power can blow lives apart if not used with care. In *Calm, Cool, and Connected*, Arlene Pellicane shows us how to maximize the blessings and benefits while minimizing the dangers and deceptions. In a world jam-packed with all things digital, this book is a must read!

PAM FARREL
Codirector, Love-Wise; author of *Men Are Like Waffles, Women Are Like Spaghetti* and *10 Best Decisions a Parent Can Make*

CALM, COOL, AND CONNECTED

5 Digital Habits
for a More Balanced Life

ARLENE PELLICANE

MOODY PUBLISHERS

CHICAGO

All Scripture quotations, unless otherwise indicated, are taken from the Holy Bible, New International Version®, NIV®. Copyright © 1973, 1978, 1984, 2011 by Biblica, Inc.™ Used by permission of Zondervan. All rights reserved worldwide. www.zondervan.com. The "NIV" and "New International Version" are trademarks registered in the United States Patent and Trademark Office by Biblica, Inc.™

Scripture quotations marked NKJV are taken from the New King James Version. Copyright © 1982 by Thomas Nelson. Used by permission. All rights reserved.

Scripture quotations marked NLT are taken from the Holy Bible, New Living Translation, copyright © 1996, 2004, 2007, 2013, 2015 by Tyndale House Foundation. Used by permission of Tyndale House Publishers, Inc., Carol Stream, Illinois 60188. All rights reserved.

Scripture quotations marked NRSV are from the New Revised Standard Version of the Bible, copyright 1989, by the Division of Christian Education of the National Council of the Churches of Christ in the USA. Used by permission. All rights reserved.

Scripture quotations marked ESV are from The Holy Bible, English Standard Version® (ESV®), copyright © 2001 by Crossway, a publishing ministry of Good News Publishers. Used by permission. All rights reserved.

Scripture quotations marked KJV are taken from the King James Version.

Edited by Annette LaPlaca
Interior Design: Ragont Design
Cover Design: Erik M. Peterson
Author photo: Anthony Amorteguy
Cover photo of woman holding phone copyright © 2016 by Javier Pardina / Stocksy (1048985). All rights reserved.

Library of Congress Cataloging-in-Publication Data

Names: Pellicane, Arlene, 1971- author.
Title: Calm, cool, and connected : 5 digital habits for a more balanced life
    / Arlene Pellicane.
Description: Chicago : Moody Publishers, 2017. | Includes bibliographical
    references.
Identifiers: LCCN 2017018853 (print) | LCCN 2017030561 (ebook) | ISBN
    9780802496140 | ISBN 9780802496133
Subjects: LCSH: Technology--Religious aspects--Christianity. | Smartphones. |
    Social media. | Time management--Religious aspects--Christianity.
Classification: LCC BR115.T42 (ebook) | LCC BR115.T42 P45 2017 (print) | DDC
    261.5/2--dc23
LC record available at https://lccn.loc.gov/2017018853

We hope you enjoy this book from Moody Publishers. Our goal is to provide high-quality, thought-provoking books and products that connect truth to your real needs and challenges. For more information on other books and products written and produced from a biblical perspective, go to www.moodypublishers.com or write to:

Moody Publishers
820 N. LaSalle Boulevard
Chicago, IL 60610

1 3 5 7 9 10 8 6 4 2

Printed in the United States of America

To my mentor Pam Farrel,
with gratitude for investing in me and so many others.
You are an example of living generously,
connecting people to God and to each other.

Contents

Foreword

We are living in rapidly changing technological times. The vast majority of Americans—95 percent—own a cellphone of some kind. Seventy-seven percent of those are smartphones, which is more than double the number reported in 2011. Phones are everywhere—in the pockets of middle schoolers, among the rich and the poor, constantly present in the home.

Children do not possess the self-control to be given carte blanche with smartphones and iPads. Left unattended, they would probably play video games or watch TV most of the day. Arlene Pellicane and I wrote about the importance of clear boundaries in a child's life in our book *Growing Up Social: Raising Relational Kids in a Screen-Driven World*. I'm glad Arlene has continued to expand our work with this new book geared for adults about our technology use.

Turns out that like children needing boundaries, we too need guiding principles and wisdom when it comes to screen consumption. Many men and women are spending hours each day watching TV on demand, scrolling through social media, noting the number of likes they receive on photos, and staring down at smartphones. This overuse and overdependence on technology leads to loneliness and isolation. In order for the love languages to flourish, we must put our devices down and speak words of affirmation. We must check our phones less and touch our spouses more. We must spend quality time with our loved ones without screens and give meaningful gifts that don't require Wi-Fi. We need less gaming time and more serving time.

I do want to assure you that Arlene isn't going to make you go cold turkey or trade in your smartphone for a dumber model (although that could be a good idea). I know she owns a smartphone, a desktop computer, and a laptop. This book isn't about getting rid of your devices. It's about gaining control over them and putting them into the proper place in your life.

There are many things you do very effectively with technology, like texting. You can tell a loved one things like "I'm parked here" or "I'll pick you up at 7." But the bulk of relationship building happens face to face. You can't hug a spouse, parent, friend, or child through the cellphone. You can't look into the face of a child through a text. You can't build trust through likes alone.

Reading this book may lead you to apologize to family members, friends, or a coworker for ignoring them while obsessing over emails, video games, or online shopping. It's never too late to start doing what is healthy. That's true on the individual level and it's also true on the family level. If you have children living in your house, it's not too late to become more actively involved in modeling and training healthy behaviors with screen time.

Technology does have many good uses and can strengthen relationships when used intentionally, moderately, and cautiously. This book you are holding will help you form healthy habits around your devices. The steps are simple but the results can be quite profound in improving your most important relationships with God and the ones you love.

GARY CHAPMAN
Author of *The 5 Love Languages*

Introduction

It Is Well
with My Phone

Our God is in heaven; he does whatever pleases him. But their idols are silver and gold, made by human hands. They have mouths, but cannot speak, eyes, but cannot see.

PSALM 115:3 – 5

Imagine a small device that has gone from nonexistent to indispensable in less than a decade. You've probably guessed it. That amazing little invention is the smartphone. As recently as 2011, only a third of Americans owned one.[1] I was a late adopter, carrying around a flip phone for years. I remember talking to my husband, James, about getting a smartphone. Practical and to the point, he asked, "Why do you need one?"

"Um," I mumbled, like a busted teenager. "When I'm out with my friends, it's embarrassing when I don't have one. They all take pictures with their phones, and I don't. I hope they don't notice that I keep my (clunky, antiquated, mortifying) phone in my purse."

"Nope, that doesn't seem like a good reason," James counseled.

Months later, when I realized I could take credit card sales for my books over my phone, I knew I had a legitimate reason. We drove to the store and began the oh-so-blissful (not) experience of buying a phone and calling plan.

I held my shiny new object, bursting with pride of ownership. Finally, I had arrived! I set it down at my desk and proceeded to work. A few seconds later, I picked up the new phone. Had anyone texted me? Should I install an app? It didn't take long for me to figure out that this phone could really mess with my productivity and personal relationships if I wasn't careful.

One of my son's teachers says, "The smarter the tablet, the dumber the student." There's certainly a kernel of truth in that. We've come to expect more from our technology and less from ourselves. If I can look up meanings to words in an instant, why should I bother learning vocabulary? If my GPS will take me to a destination, why bother getting any bearings?

Perhaps you're old enough to remember what life was like before the advent of smartphones. Or maybe you're young enough only to know a world populated by cellphones and tablets. Like other tools, they can be used to enhance your life or to make your life miserable. You're reading this book, which tells me you crave more balance in your life. You don't want to be texting at red lights, constantly scrolling through social media, and clicking for just one more email. Technology's pace is quick, and it's easy to feel as if you've got to keep up. You can become like the proverbial hamster spinning in a wheel—a hamster holding a phone like its life depended on it.

Maybe you don't feel like you're running 24/7 on a techno-crazed treadmill. You just know you'd love to text less and talk more to your spouse. You'd like to learn how to enjoy a sunset without having to take a picture of it. You'd like to look into your child's eyes instead of their hair as they hunch over a video game. If you're willing to make a few simple changes, it can be well with your phone. We must measure our dependence on our devices from time to time to make sure we aren't making idols out of them. It's more desirable to be Wi-Fi-poor but soul-rich.

The Halfway Life Is Not for You

No one wakes up on January 1st and declares from the rooftops, "I want to live a mediocre life!" You probably know *mediocre* means "moderate or low quality, not very good, ordinary, so-so." Think of the average American home, restaurant, place of worship, or workplace. It's sad that our social landscape reveals many people in "moderate or low quality" relationships, largely due to the distraction of technology.

The word *mediocre* comes to English from the Middle French, which took it from a Latin word meaning "halfway up a mountain."[2] Picture that. There's nothing wrong with being halfway up a mountain as long as you don't stay there. But too many become comfortable in the land of mediocre, stopping halfway up the mountain.

It's a *mediocre* meal when everyone around the table is looking down at cellphones.

It's a *mediocre* marriage if you text more often than you talk.

It's a *mediocre* home if your children spend more time watching TV than interacting with you.

It's a *mediocre* career when you waste time each day checking email and reading nonwork-related articles.

The halfway life is not for you. You can shake off mediocre thinking and living. A Nielsen report reveals Americans devote more than ten hours a day to screen time, and that number is growing. About 94 percent of adults have an HD television and the average adult in the United States spends about 4.5 hours a day watching shows and movies.[3]

Each of us, whether single or married, rich or poor, employed or unemployed, gets 168 hours a week to use. Let's say forty hours go to work, forty-nine hours go to sleeping (estimating seven hours per night), and two hours a day go to personal care like bathing and eating. That leaves sixty-five hours per week for all other activities. If adults are spending more than fifty hours a week with media for entertainment purposes, you can see how little time would be left for much else.

How can you quickly tell what someone values? Look at the way he or she uses time and money. Does your daily schedule reflect the values you hold dear? Are you using your spare time to pursue what you believe is important? Are you putting too much money into an entertainment system or the newest phone (even though your old one works just fine)? A life dominated by screens is a halfway life. You may say screens don't have a hold on you, but what do your habits say?

For Better or For Worse

The journey toward a more balanced digital life begins with what you do when you're operating on autopilot.

We are all creatures of habit, for better or for worse. Habits make life better or worse depending on what habits you practice. You wake up and read the Bible first thing in the morning? Good habit! You get home from work and turn on the TV immediately? Bad habit.

What is a habit anyway? Simply stated, a habit is something you do so often it becomes easy. It's a behavior you keep repeating without giving it any thought. It's how you live on autopilot.

Researchers say more than 40 percent of the actions people perform each day aren't due to conscious decision making. They are actions performed as habits.[4] Our brain chunks information together to automate what is repeated. Remember the first time you tried to type on a keyboard? I do! I was in junior high, and Mrs. Rupert was my typing instructor. J-J-J. K-K-K. L-L-L. I typed the home row over and over. Each letter of the alphabet required me to think hard and concentrate. Now I don't have to think at all about where the letters are. I just type like a machine. As my pastor Jeff Brawner once said, "Everything is difficult until it becomes easy. We shape our habits, and then our habits shape us."[5]

Charles Duhigg, author of *The Power of Habit: Why We Do What We Do in Life and Business,* diagrams the habit in a three-part loop: cue, routine, reward. The cue is a trigger that tells your brain to go into autopilot mode and which habit to use. Then comes the routine, the behavior itself, which can be physical, mental, or emotional. Finally, there's the reward, which helps your brain decide if this particular behavior is worth repeating.[6]

Let's apply this loop to how you relate to a smartphone being charged on your nightstand. You wake up in the morning and see your phone (the cue). You pick it up to see if you received any texts or emails in the night (the routine). You get a spurt of dopamine as you see the funny photo your friend sent you (the reward). As you get on with the day, maybe the thought occurs to you, "I really should read my Bible first thing, but I just never seem to do it." You may or may not relate it to that smartphone habit loop.

Charles Duhigg suggests just changing one element of the three-part loop of habit as a way to take a step toward change. You might change the cue by moving your phone to the kitchen to charge overnight. If you place your Bible where your phone was on the nightstand, you've created a new cue. When you wake up and instinctively reach for your phone, your Bible will be there instead. See how that could easily become your new morning routine? As you identify the cues and rewards that drive unwanted behaviors, you'll be able to make small switches to trick your brain into forming new, better habits.

Calm, Cool, and Connected

Changing autopilot behaviors becomes a path toward upgrading the mediocre life for a life that's calm, cool, and connected. Look for five new habits, based on the word *habit* as an acronym, in the chapters ahead. Some of these will be easy for you, though others may take more determination. Thinking creatively about changes to cues, routines, and rewards will help make these new practices easier as you move toward a calm, cool, and connected lifestyle.

Calm in the Storm

Whether you're wading into the daily news or your sister's toxic relationships, the overload of information on your phone can become like a personal storm. A frenetic pace of activity too easily becomes the norm. We'll move toward becoming more composed, quiet, and peaceful rather than being tossed about emotionally and mentally.

Cool under Pressure

Wouldn't you like to, most of the time, think and act in a rational way, not overly affected by strong feelings? It can feel good to eliminate the temptation to send texts in anger or tweet venom. The other meaning of cool that works is *very good,* as in "Those are cool shoes." Wouldn't it be cool to live totally free from phone addiction and mindless media? Very good!

Connected to God and to Others in Your Most
Important Relationships

To be connected is to be joined or linked together. Staying in close relationship with people is hard—harder than relating to media devices. Do you know people who seem more joined to their devices than they are to their family members? When human relationships get difficult—and they often do—it may just feel easier to default to devices, which are so much easier to manage. Your phone doesn't disagree with you and does exactly what you ask it

23

to (usually). The phone provides an illusion of connection, but in reality, its overuse leads to isolation.

As you begin to investigate the five new habits, let these two *No* statements guide you to make the most out of your journey toward a calm, cool, and connected lifestyle.

No Excuses

You may be tempted to make excuses or to blame others—that's just human nature. You might find yourself justifying your screen time by sayings things like, "I don't watch that much TV," or "Compared to everyone else in my office, I'm really good with email," or "That won't work for my family." Don't kill creativity with excuses. Excuses keep too many stuck halfway up the mountain. Stay open to change.

No Condemnation

Don't beat yourself up over your digital habits. For sure, I don't want to condemn you for them! This book is not about "Shame on you." It's more about "Shame off you." Sometimes good guilt comes into play—the kind that says, "I'm doing something wrong, and I'm sorry about it." That kind of conviction can move us to make positive changes to reconcile with others. Bad guilt says, "I'm terrible at this.

I'll never change." Please hear this: There is no condemnation in Christ Jesus (Rom. 8:1). Author Philip Yancey writes, "The sense of guilt only serves its designed purpose if it presses us toward the God who promises forgiveness and restoration."[7]

You're ready to begin! It's time to dial down your current digital pace to get to a better personal and interpersonal place. Remember one of Aesop's most famous fables: the tortoise was slower than the hare, but the tortoise had the reserves to finish the race first!

Quiz

HOW CALM, COOL, AND CONNECTED ARE YOU?

Here's your chance to assess whether you're Ninja Calm, Barely Calm, or somewhere in between. Mark YES or NO to the following questions, as honestly as possible.

1. Do you sometimes lose track of time when scrolling through social media or websites, or watching TV?
   ___ Yes   ___ No
2. Do others in your life occasionally complain about the amount of time you spend on technology?
   ___ Yes   ___ No
3. Do you check your phone first thing in the morning?
   ___ Yes   ___ No
4. Have you ever opted to watch TV, play video games, or answer emails on your own rather than interact with a friend or family member? ___ Yes   ___ No
5. Do you find yourself answering texts even if it means interrupting what you are already doing?
   ___ Yes   ___ No

6. Do you think your use of technology decreases your productivity? ___ Yes ___ No

7. Do you watch TV, use the computer, or check your phone late at night? ___ Yes ___ No

8. Do you often use the phone during meals or eat in front of the TV? ___ Yes ___ No

9. Have you ever changed vacation plans because of Wi-Fi availability? ___ Yes ___ No

10. Do you correspond with some online-only friends more than people you actually see in real life? ___ Yes ___ No

11. Do you have three or more active social media accounts you use daily? ___ Yes ___ No

12. If someone asks to have a talk, do you keep your phone close in case it vibrates? ___ Yes ___ No

13. Do you have your phone next to your bed or pillow when you sleep?___ Yes ___ No

14. Do you check your email more than twenty times day? ___ Yes ___ No

15. Not counting at work, do you spend more than four hours a day using electronic media such as TV, video games, phones, or tablets? ___ Yes ___ No

16. Do you feel behind and overwhelmed on most days with all you have to do? ___ Yes ___ No

17. When you have free time, do you use the phone or another device to relax? ___ Yes ___ No

18. Do you sometimes regret something you watched online or on TV, or something you posted on social media? ___ Yes ___ No
19. Do you find it difficult to sit through church without touching your phone? ___ Yes ___ No
20. On your day off, would it be hard for you to refrain from all electronic media? ___ Yes ___ No

Count your YES answers to give yourself an idea of how much change you might need to pursue in order to reach Calm, Cool, and Connected.

If you answered YES to 3 questions or fewer, you are *Ninja Calm, Cool, and Connected.* You have a great ability to balance technology and being fully present. You may want to loan this book to a friend who texts while you're together.

If you answered YES to 4 to 9 questions, you are *Almost Calm, Cool, and Connected.* You haven't gone overboard with technology, but you can easily get swept away by screen madness. Work on building a few positive habits by setting limits on your screen time. Your relationships will be healthier, and you'll be much happier as a result.

If you answered YES to 10 to 14 questions, you are *Barely Calm, Cool, and Connected.* Warning lights are flashing. You are spending too much time looking at a screen. There are more important things to do—like being with loved ones, getting a good night's sleep, and having fun without the help of technology. Make the decision to scale back your screen time before it dominates your life.

If you answered YES to 15 or more questions, you are *Nowhere Near Calm, Cool, and Connected*. Red alert! Your phone is in your pocket or within three feet at all times because you love that thing. Without the constant stimulus of your phone and other screens, you'd feel anxious. You don't do quiet very well; this book will really help you create distance between you and your phone, so you can get closer to the people you care about most.

1

H = Hold Down the Off Button

Be still, for this is a holy day.

NEHEMIAH 8:11

The lunchroom was crowded at the retreat, filled with hundreds of women laughing and eating together. We were seated around long rectangular tables. As I glanced around the room, I realized something was missing. I double-checked to make sure I was seeing right.

There were no phones on the tables. Not one.

Usually when people sit down for a meal, many will place their phone next to their plate, in a corner, or at the center of the table. It's not meant to be rude; it's just a habit to keep your phone nearby and in plain sight (and out of your pocket so it won't fall out).

Yet throughout the entire gymnasium-turned-lunch-room, there were no phones on the tables. I decided I'd better leave mine in my purse!

With no screens present, ladies in their sixties and seventies chatted away—and so did young women in their twenties. I had to smile. It was a beautiful sight. But my memory jumped back in comparison to another women's event I'd recently attended, where many women were distracted while on their phones, missing opportunities to get to know one another.

Nobody means for it to happen this way, but sometimes we hold our phones too close, too often, and too tightly—and sometimes we miss the beauty of everyday interactions with both strangers and the ones we love the most. At that retreat where the phones were safely tucked away in purses, social interaction wasn't centered around devices. The focus was centered around people. Those ladies didn't need a digital pacifier to help them communicate. They looked quite comfortable, sans screens, in the presence of one another.

It's not that these women didn't use or enjoy their phones. I'm sure they did! They had simply chosen to put them aside until a later time. They practiced the first calm, cool, and connected HABIT, the "H," which stands for "Hold Down the Off Button." They exhibited the self-control that empowers *you* to master your devices, and not let the devices master you.

Silence Is Golden

I woke up to the sound of loud music coming from downstairs. This is pretty normal, as my husband, James, often gets up earlier than I do to exercise. I prefer to stay in bed! I walked downstairs to begin making the morning smoothie. Our blender is so loud that I literally put on headphones to protect my ears. A few minutes later, the kitchen is filled with three kids' voices and the commotion of making lunches. Bikes are taken down from their hooks in the garage, and we're off to school in a blur of activity. Biking home alone, I take a deep breath and enjoy the solitude of the short ride.

When was the last time you were quiet, even just for one minute straight (and sleeping doesn't count!)? Technology at our fingertips has transformed the way we think, create, and receive information. Emails, texts, posts, articles, and likes are ever-present, many of them signaling their arrival with a beep of notification. Screens light up restaurants, airports, churches, minivans, and even gas station pumps. Digital presence is almost unrelenting. And we know that too much noise can produce stress and tension in the body. The prefrontal cortex of the brain—the part that's involved in decision making and problem solving—can get overloaded by the demands of an always-on digital life.

By the seventh day God had finished the work he had been doing; so on the seventh day he rested from all his work. Then God blessed the seventh day and made it holy, because on it he rested from all the work of creating that he had done.
GENESIS 2:2–3

Here's some good news: research indicates that silence has the opposite effect. Silence releases tension in the brain and body, producing a calmer, cooler you. One study based on changes in blood pressure and blood circulation in the brain revealed that two minutes of silence is more relaxing than listening to calming music.[1] When your brain is idle and external noise is eliminated, you can more readily tap into your inner thoughts, emotions, memories, and ideas.

I was surprised recently when I dialed up a customer service department and a recorded voice gave me the choice between hold music or silence. The digital voice said, "In silence, maybe you'll think of your next big idea." My coauthor of *Growing Up Social*, Dr. Gary Chapman, offers this in praise of being still: "Life has to be balanced. Most of life is going to be scheduled, but there needs to be some time when you don't have to be doing anything. There's a place for getting a bucket of water and putting a stick in it, and stirring it around."[2]

Picture yourself sitting next to that bucket of water, with nothing to do except stir a stick around. Imagine the quiet. See the water swishing around. Sitting like this—no agenda, no deadlines, no pressure—seems fairly foreign in our do-it-all and do-it-now world.

Past generations seem to have made a clearer delineation between work and leisure time. My family enjoys watching old TV shows like *Little House on the Prairie*. Michael Landon's character, Charles Ingalls, worked hard in the day and played his fiddle in the family room at night. He could sit at his doorway quietly after his children went to bed and replenish his spirit before another workday.

Then people go out to their work, to their labor
until evening. PSALM 104:23, emphasis mine

That sounds pretty idyllic now, doesn't it? We don't do this anymore because we can work virtually anywhere and anytime because of the computers in our pockets or just a step away. This round-the-clock access is both a blessing and a curse. To enjoy more of the blessings, we must schedule in times of rest from the noise. We must be capable of setting limits and sticking with them.

Nighttime Calm

When my daughter Noelle was two, she loved sucking her thumb at night. She didn't need a binky; she had a built-in pacifier. Her tiny thumb would be fraught with teeth marks and peeling skin. We tried painting her nails with nail polish that tasted terrible. She continued chomping undeterred. We promised rewards if she would stop. But night after night, she would suck on that little thumb like her life depended on it.

One day James came up with an unconventional plan. He took her pajama top, which was a little too long for her, and he sewed up the sleeves. When Noelle slipped her arms in her pajamas that night, she looked for her beloved thumb. But it was nowhere to be found! Like boxing gloves over her precious thumbs, the sewed up pajamas had taken away her usual pacifier for the night.

Noelle cried, sucking on her whole fist underneath her sealed pajamas. But after a few nights without access to her precious thumb, she got used to it. After a month or two, she returned to pajamas with normal sleeves, holes and all. Her thumbs, healed up in pristine condition, were safe at last. Noelle had been weaned off her nighttime binky.

I'm pretty sure you don't have a problem with using your thumb as a pacifier (your pajamas are safe!), but you might be awfully fond of your phone. Maybe you check your phone once or twice before dozing off. Maybe you receive texts in the middle of the night. Maybe you check the phone first thing in the morning. If these behaviors sound familiarly descriptive, you're not alone. Seventy-one percent of Americans sleep with or next to their smartphones.[3] There are some circumstances that require nighttime telephone access. Some professions require workers to be on call through the night. My husband, James, is a Realtor who manages several properties. He keeps his phone on the dresser in our room, in case a tenant has a leak or other emergency overnight.

But many of us, including me, can safely stash our phones to charge in another room while we sleep—and we'd be giving ourselves an advantage by doing this. A Time/Qualcomm poll conducted with 4,700 respondents in seven countries, including the United States, found that younger people were more likely to say, "I don't sleep as well because I am connected to technology all the time."[4] Alertness for calls or notification beeps can keep us sleeping too lightly. And when we're sleep deprived, we are less productive and prone to make errors in judgment at work and at home.

Be still, and know that I am God; I will be exalted among the nations, I will be exalted in the earth. PSALM 46:10

People have been studying productivity for more than 130 years. The earliest productivity studies were conducted in the 1880s by Ernst Abbe at the Zeiss lens laboratories. Researchers discovered that human workers are very productive up to forty hours per week, but beyond that we become less able to deliver quality work. We end up working extra hours to fix the mistakes we made when we were tired. After twenty-four hours of sleep deprivation, the parietal lobe and prefrontal cortex of the brain lose 12 to 14 percent of their glucose.[5] These are the areas of the brain that we need most for thinking, for social control, and for discerning between good and bad.

Even though your phone can be a source of joy and connection with friends, it also holds your direct connection to your work and other duties related to family and life management. Why not develop the good habit of charging your phone overnight either out of reach in your bedroom or in a different room? Like Noelle giving her overworked thumb a rest, separate yourself from your work and other responsibilities by putting some distance between you and your phone at night. You will sleep better and be more productive in the morning.

Do I Need a Digital Pacifier?

Iowa State University researchers developed a questionnaire to help you determine if you suffer from nomophobia, or the fear of being without your mobile phone. Researchers found about 58 percent of men and 47 percent of women suffer from the phobia, comparing stress levels to wedding-day jitters, trips to the dentist, or when their phones were lost, without power, or out of network.[6] Here is a sample from that questionnaire. The more statements you agree with, the higher your chance of being in need of a digital binky.

1. I would feel uncomfortable without constant access to information through my smartphone.
2. I would be annoyed if I could not look information up on my smartphone when I wanted to do so.
3. Running out of battery in my smartphone would scare me.
4. If I were to run out of credits or hit my monthly data limit, I would panic.

5. If I did not have a data signal or could not connect to Wi-Fi, then I would constantly check to see if I had a signal or could find a Wi-Fi network.

If I did not have my smartphone with me:

6. I would feel anxious because my constant connection to my family and friends would be broken.
7. I would feel anxious because I could not instantly communicate with my family and/or friends.
8. I would be nervous because I would be disconnected from my online identity.
9. I would feel weird because I would not know what to do.

De-Tethering

My oldest child, Ethan, entered middle school last year. On the first day of school, a fellow mom asked, "Has Ethan texted you yet?" I had to smile. It had only been one hour since he'd started his school day—and Ethan doesn't have a phone.

We live in the age of the ever-connected, monitoring parent. Being in constant contact may give us as parents a sense of security, but does a child really benefit from being tethered this closely to his or her parents?

Sherry Turkle, author of *Alone Together* says, "I talk to college students who've grown up with the habit of being in touch with their parents five, ten, fifteen times a day. And it's no longer Huckleberry Finn as a model of adolescence, you know, sailing down the Mississippi alone—we've developed a model of adolescence and childhood where we sail down the Mississippi together with our families in tow."[7]

I remember when my daughter Noelle was in elementary school and went away to church summer camp for the very first time. She would be away from home for three long nights. There would be no communication between parents and children unless there was an emergency. As we waved goodbye and watched the church van pull out of the parking lot, I wondered how she would do on the road trip. She gets carsick, and the twisting mountain roads might make the trip grueling for her. I had to wait a few days before finding out that, yes, the car ride *was* miserable and, yes, she did throw up once. But the huge smile on her face and the fact that she immediately started saving up for next year's summer camp told the bigger story.

For those of us who are parents, it's our job to foster our growing child's independence *from* us, not a growing dependence *on* us. Perhaps the explosion of cellphone use among children and teens is largely the result of parents, not children. We're the ones worried about watching over them. The phone has been transformed into a digital tether to help us keep tabs on children as much as it is a positive communication tool.

When I was in high school in the 1980s, I worked at a '50s-style diner. My shift would often end at midnight. Many evenings after that late shift, I walked across a busy street to my parked car and drove home. There were no mobile phones. I'd have to insert two dimes into a public pay phone if I needed to reach home. Most kids today have never seen a working pay phone. From the year 2000 to 2012, the number of pay phones dropped from 2.2 million to 243,487 in the United States because cellphones have become so prevalent.[8] The parents of yesteryear used to say, "I walked to school for miles in the snow uphill both ways." Now I tell my children, "I went to school without a phone!"

While the phone can provide a sense of security (real or imagined) about our connectedness to our kids, it can also become the young teen's immediate problem solver. Rather than work through problem-solving rationales, teens can simply text the parent to do the reasoning and solve the problems for them. Some young people have become so dependent on Google search or instant access to Mom and Dad, they don't have any idea what to do if they have to go an hour without Wi-Fi. The phone is a great tool, but we don't want our kids to fail to gain skills as problem solvers and independent thinkers. As we learn to hold down that Off button, we can show them how to discern when use of the phone is appropriate, helping them be less dependent on their phone and more confident in their problem-solving skills and personal convictions. We can help them avoid what some young people experience—actual panic when alone or without access to the Internet.

Maybe you don't have children but you are overly tethered to others with your phone. One woman I know had to tell her sister, "If I don't text you back right away, it's not because I'm mad at you. I will get back to you, don't worry!" We all could use more practice holding down the Off button. It's something we can practice together.

Wisdom on the Line

There's a fast-food advertisement my family has been passing lately. It says, "Dessert is calling, pick up!" My kids laugh as James shouts to those scrumptious cheesecakes and brownies, "Quick, hang up!" There's a time to say yes to dessert and a time to say no, right? If we picked up dessert every time we saw that sign, we'd all be about ten pounds heavier.

The digital world is like that dessert ad. *Try this new app to improve your life, pick up! You've got messages, pick up! Urgent news is waiting, pick up! Shoes on sale, pick up!* It's hard to resist that kind of insistence. We need wisdom to sort through the online world, choosing what is productive and positive. The book of Proverbs says that wisdom calls aloud, raising her voice in the public square.[9] Unlike that dessert, when wisdom is on the line, we'd better pick up.

The wisest man, Solomon, wrote that there is a time for everything and a season for every activity under the heavens.[10] If we were to apply Solomon's words to our present digital world, perhaps it would sound a little like this:

There is a time for everything technological,
And a season for every activity under your roof:
A time to take photos and a time to refrain from taking
*   photos,*
A time to text and a time for long conversation,
A time to install apps and a time to uninstall apps,

A time to limit and a time to use,
A time to watch funny cat videos and a time to read
thoughtfully in a corner,
A time to delay gratification and a time for lavish gifts,
A time to keep and a time to throw away,
A time for Facebook and a time to shut Facebook down,
A time for Skype and a time for getting on an airplane,
A time for digital advances and a time for silent retreat.

After the "there is a time for everything" passage, Solomon writes,

What do workers gain from their toil? I have seen the burden God has laid on the human race. He has made everything beautiful in its time. He has also set eternity in the human heart; yet no one can fathom what God has done from beginning to end. I know that there is nothing better for people than to be happy and to do good while they live. (Eccl. 3:9–12)

It feels like a good goal to "do good while we live." How can we use our phones for eternal good? How can we be calm and cool, not stressed out, with our digital usage? It begins by placing our dependence on almighty God and trusting Him with all that concerns us. We may use our phone as a GPS, but it cannot provide direction for our lives. Our phone may answer many questions within seconds, but it does not provide eternal answers apart from God. Our phone may connect us to others via text and FaceTime, but it cannot replace a hug or bread broken together. You and I are not designed to be plugged into a device 24/7. There are times to power on and times to power off.

Aiming at wiser parameters for digital use is not meant to make you feel guilty when you pick up your phone. Listen to these words from author Os Guinness: "Negative freedom is freedom from—freedom from oppression, whether it's a colonial power or addiction to alcohol oppressing you. You need to be freed from negative freedom. Positive freedom is freedom for, freedom to be. And that's what's routinely ignored today."[11]

Try not to focus on the negative habit you're trying to shake. Instead focus on the positive habit you're trying to embrace. Use your energy to put the positives into place. When you hold down the Off button of your screen more frequently, you open the door to a *freedom for. Freedom for* more spare time to kick around big ideas in your mind. *Freedom for* healthy exercise and the outdoors. *Freedom for* quality time with loved ones making memories. *Freedom for* ministering to others by listening and being present.

If by chance you've been cradling your phone a little too tightly lately, this could be the day to be *free from* your digital binky so you can be *free for* more good in your life. It begins by simply holding down the Off button.

Come to me, all you who are weary and burdened, and I will give you rest. Take my yoke upon you and learn from me, for I am gentle and humble in heart, and you will find rest for your souls. MATTHEW 11:28–29

CREATING CALM

I will not check my phone first thing in the morning. I will begin the day with a prayer, reading the Bible, exercising, or hugging a loved one.

TODAY'S PRAYER

Lord God, I do not want to rely on my phone or my screens for comfort or connection. I want to put my trust and hope in You alone. Help me let go of my digital dependence if I have been placing too much importance on my phone. You are the leader of my life. I rely on You to calm my soul today. In Jesus' name, amen.

2

A = Always Put People First

Love one another deeply, from the heart.

1 PETER 1:22

We were sitting at lunch enjoying conversation when my friend got a text. She looked at her phone and proceeded to answer the text without a word of explanation. For the next minute or two, I awkwardly looked at my nails, out the window, back at her. I was tempted to text her something like, "Hello, can we talk? After all, we are at lunch together."

Has something like this ever happened to you? While texting can certainly connect us, it can also separate us when it gets in the way of real conversation. When we are in someone else's presence, we have to train ourselves to think,

"People first. Phones second." To love someone deeply from the heart means we consider them more important than our phones. The second calm, cool, and connected HABIT is the "A," which stands for "Always Put People First."

A new command I give you: Love one another. As I have loved you, so you must love one another. JOHN 13:34

Please Look Up

In a study of fifty-five caregivers (mainly parents) eating at fast-food restaurants with children, researchers found that forty of them used a mobile device during the meal. Sixteen of those adults used their phones throughout the entire meal. No wonder some children acted out by singing or getting up to gain attention. Other children just looked straight at their caregivers, but their gaze was never returned.[1]

A different study that surveyed six thousand children found that:

- 54 percent of kids felt their parents checked their phones too often.
- 36 percent of kids said their parents' worst habit was getting distracted by their phones in the midst of a conversation.
- 32 percent of kids said this behavior made them feel unimportant.

Respondents from Brazil reported being the unhappiest as 87 percent of kids said their parents used their phones too often, and 56 percent said they would like to confiscate their parents' cellphones.[2] How's that for role reversal?

You don't have to have children to recognize that our obsession with digital devices can erode the quality of our closest relationships. Beauty is in the *eye* of the beholder, not in the *posts* of the beholder. Eye contact is a key ingredient in any healthy relationship. I remember when James and I were first dating, we would spend hours on the couch just looking at each other. We weren't even kissing yet. We called this blissful activity "face time" before there was FaceTime. That consistent eye contact connected and bonded us.

Imagine someone across the room is looking at you. If you return that gaze, it's understood as an invitation to engage in conversation. If you avert your eyes, it's interpreted as a rejection to discourage further conversation. We communicate volumes with our eyes, yet our "eye time" tends to get monopolized by screens. We stare steadily at monitors while our friends and family take the cue and move along.

We also miss opportunities to minister to strangers when our eyes are locked downward. In Acts 3:1–11, we read about a certain lame man who begged daily at the temple gate. The apostles Peter and John didn't turn away from this beggar as most temple goers did. On the contrary, different translations say they *fastened their eyes* (KJV), *looked intently* (NRSV), *directed their gaze* (ESV), *fixed they eyes* (NKJV), or *looked straight* (NIV) at the man. This posture of eye contact linked with compassion led to the lame man's miraculous healing by God. Whether we're walking into church, the workplace, or a restaurant, it's a good idea to keep our eyes open, looking up and around, not constantly looking down.

We must also lift our eyes up to God. The psalmist writes, "I lift up my eyes to you, to you who sit enthroned in heaven . . . our eyes look to the LORD our God, till he shows us his mercy."[3] This kind of looking comprises more than a quick glance. This lifting of the eyes is intentional.

It's a steady, adoring gaze filled with longing and expectation. There is power and provision in lifting your eyes to God. You might miss a few divine conversations if you're looking down at your phone more than you are looking up to the heavens.

The Pivot

When I turn a book in to the publisher, I don't submit my chapters on papyrus leaves. Obviously, I use a computer. My kids would walk through my home office and say, "Oh Mom, that is so funny. You are writing about *Growing Up Social,* and you are staring at your screen!"

During my daytime office hours, I didn't see this scenario as hypocritical or in any way contradicting that book's message of digital moderation. But I could see the irony from my children's perspective. These moments of tension between work-life and mom-life led me to a transforming practice I call "The Pivot." You too can practice "The Pivot" whether you are texting on your phone or facing your laptop. Here's what you do:

Step 1: When you sense someone approaching you, get ready to perform The Pivot.

Step 2: Turn in your chair away from the screen and

toward the incoming human being. (If you're standing, simply lift your head from your device and turn your neck and shoulders toward your subject for optimal communication.)

Step 3: Smile and look the person in the eyes. Practice body language that states, "I am listening."

If you're texting while someone approaches you, stop texting to show common courtesy. The person you're texting can wait for a moment. Even if you look up and say, "Just let me finish this sentence, and then I'll be right with you," that's better than simply ignoring someone while he or she waits until you finish up.

My eight-year-old daughter, Lucy, loves hugs. Physical touch is definitely one of her top love languages. When she walks to my desk, I employ The Pivot and turn toward her before she reaches me. I'll greet her with a big hug. After this positive attention, she'll happily trot off to do homework. That whole interaction probably takes less than thirty seconds.

But when I don't turn for that hug and Lucy has to wait for me at my desk while I finish a sentence or two, the interaction takes much longer and is much less satisfying for both of us. I'm frustrated by the interruption, and she's frustrated by being put off. The Pivot move is simple and doesn't take long, but it communicates volumes to the recipient. Turning away from your screen to turn toward your friend or family member proclaims, "You are more valuable to me than a piece of hardware." The more you notice others, the more fully alive you become.

Your Spouse Is More Interesting Than Your Phone

One husband tells me he and his wife used to read together in bed, cuddle, and talk before bedtime. Now his wife holds her phone, eyes glued to the screen, as he turns off her light. Another woman tells me her husband plays video games nonstop in his free time. She must constantly compete for his attention. Another man shares his concern about his wife, who texts during date nights and consults social media before consulting him.

Be devoted to one another in love. Honor one another above yourselves. **ROMANS 12:10**

My friend, your spouse is more interesting and important than your phone!

The average person in America checks his or her phone forty-six times a day.[4] Most people check their phones when shopping, watching television, and during leisure time. Think what would happen in your marriage if you reached out to touch your spouse as many times as you reached out to touch your phone. You might experience a romantic revolution!

It's true that your phone can connect you to your spouse. Studies show a loving text during the day can boost your affection for each other, with the biggest benefit going to the one sending the message.[5] But the phone can't hug you, hold you, lock eyes with you, or kiss you. These physical acts of affection produce the important bonding hormone oxytocin. Spending time holding your phone close can't produce oxytocin; only real human contact can do that.

I don't think any of us decides, "I'm going to ruin my marriage by giving too much attention to my smartphone, tablet, TV, or video game console." No, it's a slow slide of gradually building new habits with our screens. If you feel jealous of your spouse's phone, tablet, or TV, say so. Don't yell, accuse, or "guilt" your spouse. Simply say, "I am jealous for you. I feel invisible when I am around you, and I don't want to be invisible. I want to be here for you. I want to be your best friend and lover. What can we do to turn off our screens earlier and do more things together?"

Your spouse may not be aware of your feelings. Or perhaps your spouse hesitates to have this conversation with you. Remember, your spouse is more interesting than your phone (and if you don't agree, you're not asking your spouse the right questions).

The Return of Etiquette

The Merriam-Webster dictionary defines *etiquette* as "the rules indicating the proper and polite way to behave."[6] I'm afraid many customary codes of conduct in our society could be labeled ENDANGERED. Things like:

- Children greeting adults with a respectful handshake and eye contact
- The absence of profanity in public conversations
- The family mealtime sans video games or television
- Sitting up and paying attention to a speaker or teacher

Most courtesies begin with putting others' needs before our own. It is time for new rules of etiquette to emerge that embrace the existence of technology while retaining courtesy and proper decorum for one another. You can practice these "people first" principles in the following situations:

When You Meet Someone

Drop your device down or pivot away from your screen and look the other person in the eyes. Give the person a handshake, hug, nod—whatever you feel is an appropriate greeting. Teach children to look up and introduce themselves with a smile. Put the emphasis on the other person, and instruct children to move past shyness in order to show care for the new person. Bonus points if your children can go on to ask the adult a question like "What do you do for a living?" or "What are your hobbies?"

About a year ago, James was at a child's birthday party doing that awkward circle around the backyard, looking for someone to talk to. Intending to strike up a conversation, he landed next to another dad. The entire time James was talking and asking questions, the other man stared at his smartphone, not looking up even once at James. The conversation eventually petered out.

Do nothing out of selfish ambition or vain conceit. Rather, in humility value others above yourselves. PHILIPPIANS 2:3

When You're Eating with Friends or Family

If you want to take a picture of the food, do it quickly, and then treat your phone like a hot potato. Put it away. Do not keep it in your hands. Do not touch it. Enjoy the company of your friends and family without needless interruptions. By practicing this common courtesy, you will join in a happy minority. A study of diners in restaurants showed that 81 percent of Americans spend time looking at their phones while eating.[7]

If you live with others, one of the best decisions you can make is to have mealtimes without screens—no screens at the table, no television in the background. Not only is that good for family connectivity, it can even be good for your waistline (how's that for a surprise?). One study indicates that kindergarteners who watched TV during dinner were more likely to be overweight by the time they were in third grade. Studies show that mealtime conversation boosts the vocabulary of young children even more than being read aloud to. Teens who eat regularly with their families get better grades, are emotionally healthier, and less likely to be involved in risky behaviors like drugs or alcohol.[8]

Why is mealtime so sacred in a family's life, now more than ever? We no longer farm together or work alongside our children, as families often did in earlier times. The dinner table is the premiere place for a family to connect and find out what is happening in one another's lives. We can't waste mealtime! The silence that ensues when everyone is looking at devices would squander that opportunity. Instead we can enjoy the warmth of conversation, whether it concerns the low light of the day or a funny story.

When You're Making Comments Online

Have you noticed comments are getting snarkier? The online world allows a rudeness our grandparents would not be able to comprehend. Words you wouldn't dream of saying to someone's face, you might now type onto a screen without compunction or consequence. Please understand: it's absolutely okay to disagree with an article, blog post, or video and make a comment. But it's not okay to use profanity or name calling or to belittle the person's opinion or work.

Napoleon Hill said, "Think twice before you speak, because your words and influence will plant the seed of either success or failure in the mind of another."[9] Today you can adapt that to "Think twice before you post." Remember that on the other side of any online avatar or article is a human being, with feelings and challenges like your own.

When You Are at Work

What do you do first thing at work? If you're like me, you check your emails. Yet many productivity experts recommend pushing off emails until later in the day, choosing to tackle your most important projects first while your brain is fresh.

The eighth commandment, "Do not steal," may conjure up images of robbers stealing cash or someone snatching a giant diamond ring. But have you ever thought you might be stealing time from your employer by wasting time online when you should be working? This applies to the self-employed also (you're stealing from yourself).

One study showed that 89 percent of respondents admitted to wasting time at work each day, with 61 percent admitting to wasting thirty minutes to an hour per day. That may not seem like much, but just thirty minutes a day amounts to 130 hours each year.[10] Be responsible with your time on the job. By being faithful to your employer, you will be known for good works that glorify your God in heaven (Matt. 5:16). And if that isn't reason enough, you'll also be the kind of employee more likely to survive the next round of layoffs.

When You Arrive Home

Many people find themselves under one roof with others, but still feeling, at least in a practical way, as if they live alone. One person is working on a computer in the office. Another is watching TV in the living room, while another is wearing earbuds. Of course it's convenient for each person in the family to unwind with screens as each sees fit, but this atmosphere can be devastatingly isolating. When you arrive home, don't plug into screens, plug into people. If you live by yourself, have non-screen rituals you enjoy such as a walk around the block, cooking, or five minutes of quiet time.

When You Go to Bed

Unless you need your phone overnight for work emergencies, leave your phone outside the bedroom. You don't need your digital security blanket to fall asleep. On the contrary, the blue light of the screen can inhibit the production of melatonin, which helps you sleep, and disrupts your circadian rhythms. The health risks of electromagnetic radiation from cellphones are not fully known. It appears that phones give off such small doses that they are perfectly safe to handle, yet there are warnings that exposure near the head, especially for children, may be a health risk. To be on the safe side, simply charge your phone in a different room overnight.

If you're thinking you can't possibly go to sleep without your phone nearby, tell yourself you can do it—and try! Try this experiment for a week: Charge your phone in another room and don't check it as the last act of the day. Read from the Bible instead, pray, or jot down three things you're thankful for. If you're going to bed next to a spouse, be together, screen free. There are more important matters of the heart to mull over before bedtime.

Feedback Welcome

Have you ever had someone begin a conversation with you like this:

"I've been wanting to talk with you. Lately you've been on the phone or computer all the time . . ."

Uh-oh, right? Reflectively we become defensive and think up a list of excuses. *Work has been really busy lately. The person I'm texting is going through a tough time and really needs my help right now. I'm not the only one on the phone around here.*

Stop yourself before you settle on a solid alibi. Welcome the feedback. Truth is, we all want to put people ahead of our technology. We don't want our friends and loved ones feeling like second fiddles compared to our phones. Maybe you're dissatisfied with the way screen time is affecting your closest relationships. That dissatisfaction can drive you to make some very positive changes.

You have a choice in the matter. Your phone can't force you to use it. The video game can't make you play. The tablet can't even power on without your permission. Take control of your devices and make the commitment to put the people in your life first.

CREATING CALM

I will pivot away from my phone or computer when someone approaches me. I will look into the person's eyes and give my undivided attention, even if the conversation only takes a few seconds.

TODAY'S PRAYER

Dear Jesus, Your disciples Peter and John looked and really saw the lame man in Acts chapter 3. Help me really see the people around me—my family members, friends, and coworkers. Help me pay attention in my relationships and make my loved ones feel valued. Forgive me for ignoring others and for being overly consumed with my tasks and technology. In Jesus' name, amen.

3

B = Brush Daily: Live with a Clean Conscience

Though you probe my heart, though you
examine me at night and test me,
you will find that I have planned no evil;
my mouth has not transgressed.

PSALM 17:3

True confessions: my thirteen-year-old son, Ethan, has on occasion gone a few days without brushing his teeth. Believe me, he was not home when this happened. He was camping with the Royal Rangers boys' group from our church. He had his toothbrush and toothpaste in a little plastic bag. But that little bag didn't see the light of day or the moon of night. He could have easily kept up his daily habit of brushing, but he was distracted with other more alluring activities—like eating s'mores. He neglected his mouth.

For most of us, brushing our teeth is an automatic habit that happens—even if we're camping! We brush because it's what we do every morning and every evening. Remember in the introduction how one study found that more than 40 percent of the actions people perform each day weren't due to decision making? The behaviors had become ingrained habits, begun and completed on autopilot, without much thought.

There's a habit that's even more important than daily teeth cleaning: having a clean *heart* before God. That's why the third calm, cool, and connected HABIT is "B," which stands for "Brush Daily: Live with a Clean Conscience." Wouldn't it be beneficial to our souls if we automatically checked our conscience at the end of the day? What if we paired a ritual—like brushing our teeth—with a quick heart check?

When the disciples asked Jesus how to pray, He taught them what we refer to as the Lord's Prayer. Part of that prayer is "Forgive us our debts, as we also have forgiven our debtors. And lead us not into temptation, but deliver us from the evil one" (Matt. 6:12–13).

Because of Jesus, you and I can start with a new slate each day, forgiven and free. You can live with a clean conscience. But we must be aware of a modern obstacle that can easily ensnare us. Our mobile phones, computers, tablets, and flat screens can lead us down subtle, unsavory paths.

Blessed is the one who heeds wisdom's instruction. PROVERBS 29:18

Post No Evil

I probably don't have to convince you that cyberbullying is a problem with teenagers, but allow me to share a few statistics:

- 52 percent of students reported being cyberbullied.
- 33 percent of teens experienced threats online.
- 7 percent of students avoided school or certain places be-cause they were afraid of being harmed in some way.[1]

Calling other people names is nothing new. I remember being called "China girl" in elementary school and hiding in the bathroom until recess was over. But today a boy or girl doesn't have to chase you around the playground to say something mean. He or she can post something unkind about you anytime, anywhere. The online world can be an ugly place, and you can now carry around those hurtful comments right in your pocket.

Just scroll through a few comments on YouTube for proof that society badly needs a filter. Even at Christian-based websites, comments can be very harsh and combative. I've read comments like:

I'm sorry, but you are so wrong!
You must be an ATHEIST!
How the heck did you draw that conclusion?
Stupid
How dare you call yourself a Christian?

Whatever others are doing, you and I need to be sure our social media isn't just social, it's courteous. Is what we post from the privacy of our computers good enough to proclaim in public? Would we post the exact same words about someone if he or she were in the room with us, face-to-face?

What we post about others isn't the only problem. We can post some very negative things about ourselves. According to a social media survey, women wrote more than five million negative tweets in 2014. Four out of every five negative beauty tweets from women were about *themselves*.[2]

When my daughter Noelle was two, she stopped right in front of a full-length mirror in SeaWorld's bathroom.

She pointed to herself and proclaimed, "I look good!"

"Noelle," I asked. "Did you just say you look good?"

"Yes, Mom, I look good!"

That totally cracked me up. At age two, we girls still feel good about our appearance. At twenty, we're not so sure anymore, and at forty, we say, "Good grief! More makeup!" Yet Psalm 139:14 assures us that we are "fearfully and wonderfully made; your works are wonderful, I know that full well." When we post negatively about our appearance, we are discounting what God says about us. Just as a parent defends the beauty and worth of a child, God defends you and finds you infinitely valuable. Don't ever trash what God calls a treasure.

Brush daily by posting no evil online about others or yourself. Practice taking a moment before you post something. Be especially careful about posting something when you are angry or upset. If you post something and then regret making the post, take it down, and remember, you can apologize! (To learn more about the art of apology, I recommend *When Sorry Isn't Enough* by Gary Chapman and Jennifer Thomas).

We demolish arguments and every pretension that sets itself up against the knowledge of God, and we take captive every thought to make it obedient to Christ. 2 CORINTHIANS 10:5

Avoid the Poison of Pornography

The stigma once associated with going to a seedy adult store to view pornography no longer exists. Porn can be accessed by anyone in the privacy of home or anywhere with a mobile device or tablet. The late Dr. Adrian Rogers, pastor and teacher of Love Worth Finding Ministries, wrote:

It's as though a sewer pipe has broken open. And tragically we seem to be getting immune to it! What was horrible yesterday is acceptable today and a stepping-stone for something worse tomorrow. Pornography is the idea that sex can be divorced from love, from morality, from responsibility, from lifetime commitment—that you can take sex alone and somehow use sex and be successful. Indeed, you cannot.[3]

Many teens and young adults have been raised with pornography not only being available, but being *acceptable.* In a Barna study, teens and young adults considered "not recycling" to be more immoral than viewing pornography! Twenty-two percent of young adults aged eighteen to twenty-four considered porn to be good for society. Nobody over age fifty thought so.[4]

My guess is those middle-aged responders knew from experience that pornography poisons the user and his or her family. According to the research of Dr. Victor Cline, emeritus professor in psychology at the University of Utah, there are four stages of pornography use:

Addiction: Pornography provides very exciting and powerful imagery. The porn consumers get hooked. They keep coming back for more.

Escalation: With the passage of time, the addicted require rougher, more explicit, more deviant sexual material to get their "highs."

Desensitization: Material originally thought of as shocking, taboo, illegal, repulsive, or immoral over time becomes seen as acceptable and commonplace. The sexual activity depicted becomes legitimized.

Acting Out: Now addicts try to act out the behaviors viewed in the pornography. This behavior frequently grows into a sexual addiction, which they are unable to break.[5]

If you are using pornography, whether it's once a year or more often, I encourage you to turn away from this devastating practice. You can find strength and help by meditating on and memorizing Psalm 119:9–11, and it would be wise to find an accountability partner. Brush your heart daily and keep a clean conscience by praying these verses aloud and doing what it says: "How can a young person stay on the path of purity? By living according to your word. I seek you with all my heart; do not let me stray from your commands. I have hidden your word in my heart that I might not sin against you."

Protection against Porn

Lynn Marie Cherry understands the deep pain of betrayal. A few days after she delivered their second child, she discovered her spouse was addicted to pornography. She and her husband, David, have walked down the road to recovery and have been married more than twenty-five years. Whether you are married or single, porn addiction is destructive to the soul. Here what Lynn writes about using the Internet accountability and filtering service Covenant Eyes:

> We were crunching numbers, trying to make room in the budget for something I can't quite recall, when I asked my husband if we still needed to pay for Covenant Eyes.
>
> We were years down this recovery road. He hadn't acted out online in a long time. I figured maybe all was well and we could eliminate this vestige of our past pain from the spending plan. I was wrong.

My husband responded quite adamantly that we still needed Covenant Eyes and would be using it for life because it helped him not give in when he was tempted.

When he was tempted? It was disconcerting to hear my husband talk about being tempted. I would like to believe that temptation was dead and buried right along with that secret life he once lived.

"So you're still tempted?" I asked. "I thought you were walking in freedom."

"Freedom is not the absence of temptation."

I walked away from the conversation evaluating my safety. And here's why I'm on board with using Covenant Eyes for life:

1. Accountability works. After forty-eight weeks of group therapy and watching the pain I walked through, my husband does not want to see that again. He knows I'll receive the weekly accountability report, and he doesn't want to hurt me. He also doesn't want to answer to his friend that is sure to follow up on anything that doesn't look right.

2. Even though it may not make sense at first glance, I am safer when my husband embraces

his weakness than when he was over confident in his own strength. He tried for many years to find freedom on his own. We know that white-knuckling it doesn't work.[6]

Just One More Purchase

Compared to porn, cyberstalking, or posting insults, going online to shop may appear very nearly harmless, right? My ten-year-old daughter asks for time on Amazon to shop for gel pens, water bottles, and penguin stuffed animals. My husband routinely has some kind of exercise equipment, air filter, book, or battery in our online shopping cart. Just writing this paragraph has reminded me to stop and shop online for makeup (I need powder).

Whether you're ordering books, shoes, flowers, or office furniture, online retailers have made shopping easy, fun, and hassle-free. Something is always on sale! But make no mistake. Advertisers know what you like to buy. They will work to grab your attention and then make you interested enough to click that Purchase button. One study found three key factors that make people especially prone to an online-shopping addiction:

- A preference for buying anonymously and avoiding social interaction
- A preference for a wide variety and constant availability of items
- A preference for instant gratification

I'll admit I like shopping in the comfort of my home without having to fight for a parking spot. I also like a wide variety of items and having my order delivered magically on my doorstep. Does that mean I have a shopping addiction? Not necessarily. Usually those who have an unhealthy relationship with online shopping feel preoccupied with shopping and as if they have no control over it. Here are five signs to look for to determine if you have a serious problem with online shopping. How many of these are true for you?

1. I feel like I can't stop online shopping even if I wanted to and/or have tried to stop without being able to.
2. Online shopping has hurt my relationships, work, or financial situation.

3. My partner, family members, or friends are concerned about my online shopping. I end up in arguments with them over it.
4. I get grumpy or upset if I can't shop online.
5. I often feel *guilty* after I go online shopping.[7]

How did you do? If you struggle with keeping your online shopping in balance, here are a few suggestions to bolster your conscience and bank account:

• Write shopping lists and stick to them.
• Avoid TV-shopping channels and online stores when you are just browsing.
• Unsubscribe from sale emails from retailers.
• Create a log—on paper or electronically—of your online purchases each month.
• Don't leave your credit card information online as a default. Make it harder to make a purchase by requiring yourself to type in the numbers each time.
• Don't go to your favorite shopping website during downtime. Put something else that feels good in the same spot: stretch, go outside, write a note, or read a book instead.

Turn my eyes away from worthless things;
preserve my life according to your word.
PSALM 119:37

Notice Others in a Selfie World

Just a decade ago, a person with a camera would spend time taking pictures of *other* people. Today we spend time taking pictures of *ourselves*: *me* at the ocean, *me* at the restaurant, *me* on vacation. You can even find the new word *selfie* in the dictionary. It was proclaimed the word of the year in 2013 by the Oxford Dictionary.[8] Selfies are everywhere. Is there any harm in all this fuss focused on self?

The constant tracking of self often leads to a growing indifference to others. The bigger we become inside the frame of our own focus, the smaller everyone else becomes. Society would benefit from a non-selfie movement of people who focus on others online. Technology can be well used to leave a legacy and to invest in people and causes you believe in.

In his book *The Me I Want to Be,* author John Ortberg writes,

> A wise man once said that just as the three laws of real estate are "location, location, location," the three laws of relationship are "observation, observation, observation." People who give life to us are people who notice us. When we work to truly observe another person, in that self-forgetfulness our own soul flourishes.[9]

Observation, Observation, Observation

When you walk into a room, do you take the attitude of "Here *I* am! Come and talk to me"? Or do you step through the doorway and think, "Ah, there *you* are! I've been wanting to find out how you are doing"? Turning our focus outward takes practice—and intention. God calls us to be observation-oriented, "There you are!" people, men and women genuinely interested in others. But we live in a "Here I am" world focused around selfies and self-centered interests. It's human nature to go online and post what makes you look good or something that will draw attention to yourself. But that continual practice is, ultimately, an empty endeavor.

John the Baptist could have been a social media sensation. A man wearing camel's hair, eating honey sticks and high-protein locusts, taking selfies with the Jordan River in the background would go viral. The Bible tells us people went to see him from Jerusalem, all Judea, and the whole region of the Jordan. He was famous. He could have successfully launched a baptism schedule app or tweeted, "Repent, for the kingdom of heaven has come near! #forerunnerofJesus."

But that's not how he rolled.

Instead John the Baptist spoke of one coming who was more powerful, whose sandals he wasn't even worthy to carry. When his disciples were troubled about Jesus because "behold, He is baptizing, and all are coming to Him!" (John 3:26 NKJV), John replied, "He must increase, but I must decrease (John 3:30 NKJV).

John the Baptist had no trouble pointing the camera toward Jesus, not toward himself. I doubt he was worried about losing his identity or popularity in the wake of the Messiah. No, just the opposite happened. When the spotlight shifted to Christ, John was delighted, proclaiming "that joy is mine, and it is now complete" (John 3:29). Jesus Himself noticed others for "even the Son of Man did not come to be served, but to serve, and to give his life as a ransom for many" (Mark 10:45).

Do you feel weary of keeping up with the Joneses or of exalting yourself so others might validate your accomplishment? Then put away your selfie stick and awaken the powers of observation, observation, observation. As you notice others and care for them, your joy will be multiplied and your conscience will be clean.

What Happens if You Don't Brush Daily?

I was kind of surprised (and grossed out) to read that half of Americans don't floss daily and one in five don't brush twice daily![10] When you don't brush your teeth regularly, bacteria build up, forming plaque. Plaque leads to tooth decay, cavities, and potentially something worse, as I learned in my twenties.

Confession time: I was an occasional flosser in my younger years. During one appointment, the dentist soberly informed me that my lower left second molar was so far gone that I should either have it pulled entirely or get an implant. The implant was awfully expensive, so as my current dentist says, "If you have to lose a tooth, the lower left second molar is a good one."

Above all else, guard your heart, for everything you do flows from it. PROVERBS 4:23

After my getting-a-tooth-yanked-out-in-my-twenties incident, I decided daily flossing would be a positive ritual to add to my life. It took that dramatic turn of events to push me to this conclusion. I use my mouth as a visual aid whenever my children are tempted to skip brushing and flossing. I just crank open my mouth and point to the gap. "Do you want this? Do you want a big hole where your tooth should be? I didn't think so. Now go brush and floss!"

In terms of moral atmosphere, the Internet can be a dangerous place with sensational news, scantily clad models, constant advertising, addicting video games, social media pressure, and the like. It's just so easy to let overexposure to these elements create a kind of buildup of moral "plaque." If you don't brush daily and keep a clean conscience before God, this moral plaque can begin to form imperceptibly on your heart and mind. Don't wait for a catastrophic problem to mend your ways, as I did in my twenties with my teeth. It's so much wiser to "brush daily," keeping a soft, humble heart before God. Heed the words found in Proverbs 4:23: "Above all else, guard your heart, for everything you do flows from it."

CREATING CALM

As I brush my teeth at night, I will ask myself, "Have I brushed my heart? Do I have a clean conscience before God?"

TODAY'S PRAYER

Dear Jesus, I join the psalmist and pray, "Search me, God, and know my heart; test me and know my anxious thoughts. See if there is any offensive way in me, and lead me in the way everlasting" (Psalm 139:23–24). I want to live with a clean conscience before You. Forgive me of my sins. I repent and turn to You. In Jesus' name, amen.

4

I = I Will Go Online with Purpose

Whatever you do, work at it with all your heart, as working for the Lord, not for human masters, since you know that you will receive an inheritance from the Lord as a reward. It is the Lord Christ you are serving.

COLOSSIANS 3:23–24

When James and I were first married almost twenty years ago, he asked me to participate in a strange and bold experiment. Could we have a TV-free home for the first month of marriage? Keep in mind I was a television producer at the time! His idea seemed extreme. But with quality time together in mind, I said yes. We ended up loving our evenings together during that first month. When the experiment was over, we missed our peaceful oasis. We decided to nix television and cable, and we've never had it since.

When I'm speaking and traveling, it's a big treat for me to sit on the hotel bed and watch TV. My favorites tend to be reruns of shows like *Everybody Loves Raymond* and *Full House*. When I choose a beloved sitcom or chick flick on the menu guide to watch, I'm good. Watching TV is a fun and relaxing activity. But when I aimlessly flip through dozens and dozens of channels, getting sucked into watching yet another hour of who-knows-what, I regret the time wasted. Just like in television, there's a difference between going online to browse and going online with purpose.

The fourth calm, cool, and connected habit is the "I" in HABIT: I will go online with purpose. You are the only one who can make this declaration. No one else can do it for you.

Ask This Question First

Before you pick up your phone or sit down to your computer, ask this clarifying, powerful question: *what am I here to do?* Practice asking it when you pick up your phone or when you come to your home computer. Be able to give a concrete answer. Your answer may be something like:

- I am going to text my friend about lunch.
- I will check my emails.
- I'm completing my report.

When you use your device without asking this question first, you end up doing things like:

- Browsing Amazon for fitness trackers and phone accessories
- Checking how much round trip airfare would be to your next travel destination
- Scrolling through Instagram
- Clicking on that sale ad
- Going on a news site

According to a University of Nevada study, such "cyberloafing" costs US business as much as $85 billion a year. In another study, people admitted to cyberloafing from 60–80 percent of their time online at work.[1] Whether we work for a traditional employer or for ourselves, we're all susceptible to digital distractions. But if you will make it a habit to go online with purpose, you'll save a ridiculous amount of time and energy.

Technology is supposed to aid you in organization and

time management, yet we often stumble aimlessly through the land of too-much-information and tantalizing head-lines. An image catches your eye. But let's be honest; you really don't need to know what your friend had for dinner or if the celebrity couple is going to split up.

What about news? That seems legitimate. But there are downsides to living in the era of the twenty-four-hour news cycle, fast-paced and always changing. Consider the newspaper of yesteryear. It was not only more content rich than television or online news, but it was confined to the breakfast table or a favorite easy chair. Catching up on the news had a beginning and ending. News is now every-where, all day long, and largely entertainment driven.

If you find yourself wasting minutes or hours on the news, try a different system to save time. You might want to go back to reading an actual newspaper. Any current event that's really important will be there. Or plan to check the news just once a day online—and preferably not first thing. Your brain is freshest as you start the day on your computer. Use that time for your harder work and leave the news for an afternoon break or later in the day.

Let's bring in our main question again. Before you enter the world of Wi-Fi, ask: *what am I here to do?* For some, making a list of priority activities the night before to start the day with purpose really helps. For others, it's scribbling out Post-it notes on the spot. Create a workable system that puts objectives and deadlines in front of you.

Go to the ant, you sluggard; consider its ways and be wise! It has no commander, no overseer or ruler, yet it stores its provisions in summer and gathers its food at harvest. PROVERBS 6:6–8

Better Done Than Started

Do you tend to dabble in this and that online, not really finishing the things you start? It's so easy to look at articles or blogs and check email, keeping busy but without necessarily becoming productive. I know I've dragged the same task over to the next day numerous times in my calendar life. What prevents me from just getting that task done in the first place? I probably returned an email, shopped online for kids' clothes, and commented on my friend's anniversary. Have you been there? Research shows every time we become distracted, it takes an average of fifteen minutes to regain complete focus. Fifteen minutes—and that's just to get back into the zone you wandered away from in the first place![2]

One secret to getting things done is batching similar activities together. By grouping similar tasks, you maximize concentration and decrease distraction. For example, I currently write devotionals. When I batch my devotional writing in one day's work, it helps me stay in the same frame of mind, which enables me to write faster. Instead of working on the devotionals a little bit here and there over a course of a week, I block a chunk of time and get them done.

My personal Achilles' heel is email. I constantly want to click on my inbox several times an hour. After all, a timely response is my goal. But if I limited checking email to three or four times a day as many business experts suggest, I'm sure my response time would still be suitable. I don't *need* to constantly check my email, and neither do most of you.

A poll shows the average worker in the United States spends 6.3 hours checking email every day. About half that time is work related and the other half is personal.[3] It doesn't take research, although the research is plentiful, to conclude that obsessively checking emails is harmful to productivity. Author Peter Bregman observes there's a reason email management has grown from zero hours per week to 28 percent of a person's time in one generation. "Email is such a seductress in terms of distraction because it poses as valid work."[4] When you don't feel like working on a proposal, inputting data, or writing your award-winning masterpiece, you can check email and appear to be working. Keep in mind, work expands to the time allotted.

You might have to try various methods to help you fight the urge to waste time online, so that you can find what works for you. You might try the Pomodoro Technique,[5] a method created in the 1980s by Francesco Cirillo, implementing the Pomodoro tomato-shaped timer as its workhorse. Here's how it works. Choose a task, either big or small, that you have been putting off. Set the Pomodoro timer for twenty-five minutes. Work on the task until the Pomodoro rings. If you think of a different task needing attention during that twenty-five minutes, jot it down on paper, then continue with your main task. When the Pomodoro rings, put a check mark on a paper. Take a short break such as getting coffee or taking a quick walk. After completing four Pomodoros (equaling a hundred minutes of productive work), you can give yourself a longer break of twenty to thirty minutes.

When you sit down to write that report or create a

killer marketing campaign, it can be overwhelming, demotivating, and stress-inducing. That's where the beauty of batching tasks and working for set periods of time comes in. You might not be able to power through all the way until 5:00 p.m., but you can certainly do twenty-five minutes of good work, right? Working strong in uninterrupted chunks of time is a great system for lawyers, accountants, managers, teachers, parents, students, writers, and workers in many other professions.

Everyone who competes in the games goes into strict training. They do it to get a crown that will not last, but we do it to get a crown that will last forever. 1 CORINTHIANS 9:25

Others may find twenty-five minutes to be limiting, preferring to work in longer chunks toward a lunch break or a dinner break. The key is finding a system that works for you to get tasks not just started, but actually get them done. Minimizing online interruptions, having a clean workspace, and building momentum can also help you get your to-do list checked off faster. Brainstorm a bit: what activities can you batch together in an average work day?

Know to Grow

A man named Buckminster Fuller created the "Knowledge Doubling Curve," noting that until 1900 human knowledge doubled approximately every century. By the end of World War II, knowledge was doubling every twenty-five years. Today the growth of knowledge is hard to calculate. Nanotechnology knowledge is doubling every two years and clinical knowledge every eighteen months. Human knowledge is said to double every thirteen months, and according to IBM, the "internet of things" will lead to the doubling of knowledge every twelve hours.[6]

The wired world is a behemoth of knowledge. How will you use it? Try not to go online just to *know* more. Set out to go online to *grow* more. There's a world of difference between simply knowing and actually growing. Many people focus on acquiring more knowledge instead of putting into practice what they already know. For example, I can watch hours of yummy-looking food on cooking shows but until I complete a recipe, it doesn't have much practical application.

I can read relationship articles all day long, but am I becoming more affectionate and respectful to my spouse by just reading?

Think about a typical day and the websites and social media places you visit. Here are a few questions to gauge your online growth chart:

- Are you learning about new tools to do your job better?
- Are your emails to the point and do they advance the completion of a project?
- Does your research help you in your presentations or product development?
- Do your online Bible study tools add depth to your reading?

Technology offers teaching to help you learn to do pretty much anything you want, from changing the oil in a car to quilting the *Mona Lisa*. Improving skills has never been cheaper or more accessible to more people. That technology is a gift when it's harnessed to serve your goals in life, not to distract you from them. Don't settle for barely getting your job done and cyberloafing the rest of the time. Be purposeful about your media use to enrich your life. Use it to grow, not just to know.

My children, who are in elementary school and middle school, are required to use computers at school and for homework. We make screen time at home very intentional. We don't surf the web; we are destination users. We want our kids to know more in order to grow more. My eighth-grader's screen reward after homework is watching a five-minute Prager University video. I fully support these short videos about big topics such as economics, history, and religion.

I do live in the real world. I understand there is a totally legitimate place for taking an online break. Facebook can be fun. Not every page visit must be educational in nature, teaching a meaningful life lesson. Cute cat videos have their place. I won't condemn you for sharing a funny video of some guy falling off a treadmill. But when you're done laughing, get back on track. We can't get stuck in the land of "Click-on" where we just keep clicking on the next suggested video, article, or website. We don't have time for that. We've got too much growing to do!

Do your best to present yourself to God as one approved, a worker who does not need to be ashamed and who correctly handles the word of truth. 2 TIMOTHY 2:15

5 Ways to Be More Efficient Online

- Use a timer and put it next to your computer. Work in chunks of time with short breaks in between.
- Keep a daily updated list of things to do and stick to the list.
- Program your computer to shut off at a certain time each evening.
- Make your computer desktop clean and organized. Use wallpaper you find inspiring and motivational.
- Listen to your best music for working.

5 Ways to Tame Your Inbox

- Don't be afraid to hit delete. Develop an anti-clutter attitude and delete with gusto.
- Use the two-minute rule. If you can do what's being requested in less than two minutes, do it immediately. This gets it off your to-do list before it ever gets on your to-do list.
- Unsubscribe from email lists. Keep a few you really like, but unsubscribe from the rest.
- Turn on "Send and Archive." Gmail has a feature called Send & Archive, which automatically archives an email thread as soon as you reply. No need to give precious real estate to these emails in the inbox.
- Search for Big Offenders. Search for emails with large attachments. Getting rid of these can free up space and increase speed.

5 Ways to Maximize Social Media

- *Allot a certain amount of time for social media.* Do you use social media for personal reasons? Fifteen minutes a day may be plenty. Need to use social media to promote your business? Maybe one hour a day will do the trick. Determine how much time per day you'll spend on social media and stick with that objective. Track your time for one week if you're having difficulty staying with it.

- *Eliminate social media during mealtimes.* Not even FaceTime can replace real human interaction. Dinner is not the time to scroll through your social media posts, even when your party is waiting for a table at a restaurant. In a Stanford University study, girls who spend much of their waking hours on social media are more likely to develop social problems. One antidote? Plenty of time interacting face-to-face with people.[7]

- *Don't look at social media first thing in the morning or at bedtime.* If you greet the day with text messages and notifications, you feel behind before breakfast.

Instead spend first minutes in prayer and reading God's Word, which is a much better way to frame your day. Likewise, drift off to sleep by counting blessings instead of counting all the emails you have to respond to the next day.

- *Participate in social media fasts.* If you would be anxious about missing out on social media for one week, you are a good candidate for a fast. Researchers are finding chemical changes in certain pleasure areas of the brain when we get that "social media hit."[8] If it's becoming addictive and disruptive to the rest of your life, a time of detox can be very healthy. You can also take one day a week off or have social media free weeknights.

- *Use it to stay connected with a handful of friends.* My parents use WhatsApp to send photos to family members overseas. When you use social media to stay in touch with just a few people, it can enhance relationships versus scrolling through news feeds to check in on the masses.

Rethinking Multitasking

My daughter Noelle was playing a game called Bop It. It was an older version that requires the player to squeeze the handles when the dancing lights enter the target zone. I asked her to unload the dishwasher. Several minutes later, I peeked in the kitchen to see Noelle still playing Bop It and unloading one dish at a time during pauses in the game. She thought herself clever to combine the activities so she didn't have to stop playing while still getting the job done. Or so she thought! Multitasking gives the illusion of working smart, but in reality, Noelle could have unloaded the dishwasher in a fraction of the time, and then returned to her game.

Seeing Noelle in the kitchen was an illuminating visual of the myth of multitasking. We think, "Wow, look at me! I'm doing two, or three, or four things at once. This is great!" But research indicates that multitasking isn't all it's cracked up to be.

Multitasking increases the amount of time it takes to do a task. According to Stanford professor Clifford Nass, today's nonstop multitasking actually wastes more time than it saves. "People who multitask all the time can't filter out irrelevancy. They can't manage a working memory. They're chronically distracted."[9] Doing several things at once drives our productivity down as much as 40 percent.[10] We're not truly multitasking; we're actually switching quickly from one thing to another, interrupting ourselves—and interruptions cost time.

Multitasking reduces the quality of your work. One study showed people who were distracted by an incoming email or phone call saw a ten-point fall in their IQs. That's similar to losing a night of sleep, and that's more than twice the effect of smoking marijuana.[11] In another experiment, students were asked to sit in a lab and complete a standard cognitive skill test. One group of subjects was not interrupted while taking the test. The other group was told they may be contacted with further instructions at any moment via text. They were interrupted twice during the exam. The interrupted group scored 20 percent lower than the other group.[12] That difference is enough to bring a B-minus student down into failure range.

Multitasking can interfere with short-term memory. When you are switching quickly from one thing to the next, you have less attention available to store memories. If you're listening to someone in conversation and texting at the same time, it may be difficult to recall the information shared in person. According to Dr. David Meyer, a professor of psychology at the University of Michigan, the flood of adrenaline and other stress hormones released when you are trying to do too many things at once can actually cause damage to the brain cells that store memories.[13]

Dear children, keep away from anything that might take God's place in your hearts. 1 JOHN 5:21 NLT

Instead of switching from thing to thing as if you're a contestant for the trophy of World's Best Multitasker, concentrate on one task at a time. Pause between switching and be fully present. Fight that inclination to open one more window. Ask yourself the key question "What am I here to do?" Resolve to go online with purpose and gusto. When we're focused, technology will serve us well, but without focus we can be led down a never-ending zigzag path.

CREATING CALM

Before turning on my computer or touching my phone screen, I will ask the question "What am I here to do?"

TODAY'S PRAYER

Dear Jesus, I don't want to waste time online or be a slave to my devices. Speak to me and give me purpose. Help me develop discernment to tell between right and wrong. Alert me to the ways I am wasting time and energy. I want to do my work with all my heart as working for You. I want my life to be filled with purpose. In Jesus' name, amen.

5

T = Take a Hike

Ask the animals, and they will teach you, or
the birds of the sky, and they will tell you;
or speak to the earth, and it will teach you, or
let the fish in the sea inform you. Which of all
these does not know that the hand of the LORD
has done this? In his hand is the life of every
creature and the breath of all mankind.

JOB 12:7–10

Let's take a short imagined trip together. I invite you to walk down on a shaded dirt path through a grove of trees, hearing nothing but the sound of God's creation. Birds chirp. Leaves stir in the wind. A sense of calm envelops your soul as you walk through the green and look up at the majestic trees. Psalm 19:1–2 tells us, "The heavens *declare* the glory of God; the skies *proclaim* the work of his hands.

Day after day they *pour forth* speech; night after night they *reveal* knowledge" (emphasis mine).

Notice the verbs in those two verses. God is communicating to us through creation, offering a silent, continual testimony to those who take the time to be still and know. It doesn't matter if you speak English or Swahili, geek or Greek, day after day and night after night, the outdoor world declares God's existence.

But in this highly digital world, it can be startlingly easy to pass through the wonder of creation without noticing anything at all. One day a teenager in my neighborhood was walking down the *middle* of the street, head down, buds in, looking at her phone. Our two-ton gray minivan pulled up a few feet behind her and—I kid you not—she didn't even know we were there. We literally followed her down our residential road until she very casually veered to the left to get on the sidewalk. Even as our vehicle drove away, she never looked up or acknowledged our presence. Yet we could have run her over.

Taking a walk around the block with face buried in a phone is *not* what I mean by the letter "T" in HABIT. The fifth and final calm, cool, and connected habit is: Take a Hike. I will go outdoors. I will notice and be refreshed in God's creation.

LORD, our Lord, how majestic is your name in all the earth! You have set your glory in the heavens. . . . When I consider your heavens, the work of your fingers, the moon and the stars, which you have set in place, what is mankind that you are mindful of them, human beings that you care for them? PSALM 8:1, 3–4

Stop Going to Your Room

"Go to your room!" was a common punishment used by yesterday's parent. This parental intervention doesn't work so well in contemporary times. Today's misbehaving child has no qualms about staying indoors confined to a room. A more effective directive might be "Go outside!"

My husband, James, tried this a few years ago. When our kids were especially rambunctious in the house, he told them all, "Go outside. Run around the block and come back." They stared at him blankly. Go outside to do what? Walk by themselves in our neighborhood? The girls started to cry, which sealed the inevitability of their outdoor excursion.

They made a big fuss as the front door shut behind them. About ten minutes later, three kids emerged, none injured by the unstructured time outdoors. In fact, they were much more agreeable after their energy had been expended. Kids thrive outside with sunshine, free play, and bodies in motion. Yet children are spending less time outdoors, mostly due to safety reasons, busy schedules, and the popularity and addictive nature of screen time.

Would you be surprised to hear that three-quarters of children in the United Kingdom spend less time outside than prison inmates? I certainly was surprised when I saw this survey that reveals the dramatic decline in outdoor play. Inmates are required at least one hour of suitable exercise in the open air daily, which is much more than most kids are getting. A fifth of the children in the UK didn't play outside at all on an average day. Another report found more than one in nine children had not set foot in a park, forest, beach, or other natural environment for at least a year.[1]

James and I had the lovely experience of speaking on a marriage cruise to the Caribbean. In Jamaica, I asked our young tour guide if kids in Jamaica play video games. To my surprise, she said because cellphones were very cheap, most kids stay indoors and play games on their phones. She said it was terrible and very different from the way she had been raised, playing outside with neighborhood kids. Holding a phone on one's lap hardly counts as physical activity. The overuse of technology is hurting kids in many countries around the world, not just America.

What about adults? According to the EPA, the average American spends 93 percent of his or her life indoors (87 percent indoors and 6 percent in cars). That leaves only 7 percent of a person's life outdoors, which translates into one half day per week.[2]

Thankfully, studies have shown getting outside and moving for as little as five minutes can improve your mood and health.[3] A walk in the woods (or just down your street) can make a positive difference. Dr. Gary Chapman says, "As adults, we can take mini-vacations during the day, five minute vacations to get up from your desk, take a walk and look out a window. Those moments are valuable."[4]

The LORD loves righteousness and justice; the earth is full of his unfailing love. By the word of the Lord the heavens were made, their starry host by the breath of his mouth. PSALM 33:5–6

Why This Homebody Got a Dog

I must admit writing about the habit of "Take a Hike" has me convicted. The Pellicane family does spend a lot of time indoors, going from school to the homework table, to martial arts, to the dinner table, to bed. I bike with my girls to school about twice a week to get outdoors. One morning, I was biking too slow, waiting for a car to back out of the driveway. Without any momentum, I started falling toward the right and, with my toe clips in, down I went. My girls gathered around me. One neighbor taking a walk asked if I wanted an ambulance. Of course, I didn't need an ambulance, but I did need an ice pack!

We were close to home so we walked our bikes back, and I drove the girls to school that morning. I iced my knee; it was hard to bend for a few days. I had a sore back too, but a good story. It can be inconvenient to go outside, but there is a sense of adventure outdoors that doesn't exist in the predictable, tame indoor world.

Maybe that's why we recently got a dog.

For our eighteenth anniversary date, James and I were walking past quaint shops when we noticed a big dog in an upscale men's clothing store. He looked like a giant teddy bear. I thought he was a stuffed animal, but James insisted he was real. We walked into the store, drawn not by the clothes, but by the dog. It turned out he was a real live goldendoodle, a lovable, smart mix between a golden retriever and a poodle.

I've never had a dog (or wanted one), but this was a rare moment. I thought, "I just might be able to own *that* dog." We spoke to the owner at length and within two weeks, we were getting a goldendoodle puppy. Why this impulsive turn of events? James was motivated by the desire to get outside. He sees we are increasingly an "indoor family," and this alarms my outdoor-loving husband. He knows a dog will force us out of the house. Dr. Richard Schwartz of Harvard Medical School says, "One of my colleagues jokes that people with dogs are the least likely to be depressed" since they always go outside to walk them in the morning.[5]

Our little puppy, Winston (as in Churchill), is helping this homebody get out more. You don't have to get a dog to get a daily dose of the outdoors, but it can certainly be a motivating factor. Perhaps you've heard the saying "Environment is stronger than willpower." It's a lot easier to stick to your weight-loss goals in a gym than it is in a bakery! Temptation with technology works the same way. If you're surrounded all day by computers, phones, tablets, and flat screens, you're going to sit like a couch potato and use them. By creating an environment that forces you outside (such as having a dog or scheduling a tennis game each week with a friend), you'll create better boundaries with your phone and other devices.

5 Good Reasons to Go Outside

- *Get Your Dose of Vitamin D.* When sunlight hits your skin, it begins a process that leads to the creation and activation of vitamin D, which fights conditions like cancer, osteoporosis, and heart attacks. My husband,

James, is known to go bare-chested for a minute or two during rest stops on road trips. You don't have to go overboard. Five to fifteen minutes of sunlight on your arms, hands, and face two to three times a week is enough to enjoy the benefits. Wear sunscreen for extended times in the sun.[6]

- *Feel Happier.* Exposure to sunlight increases the brain's release of the hormone serotonin, which is associated with boosting mood. Low levels of serotonin are associated with feeling more depressed. That's why people typically talk about the winter blues, not the summer ones.

- *Increase Your Concentration Power.* In his book *Last Child in the Woods,* Richard Louv coined the phrase "nature-deficit disorder." In a study, participants given a memory test scored better when they took a walk around an arboretum than the other participants, who walked down a city street.[7] A little bit of time looking at green spaces may be just what you need to get your mind back in gear.

- *Make Exercise Easier.* Research shows that the color green, such as found on trees in nature, makes exercise feel easier. Cyclists were tested pedaling in front of green, gray, and red images. Those exercising in front of the green reported feeling lower exertion and mood swings when biking in front of nature's green color.[8] Another study found kids were twice as active when outside than inside.[9] It's true for adults too. Less time indoors and more time outside results in more walking, gardening, biking, and other activities that make you move your body.

- *Enjoy Antiaging Benefits.* Getting outside will help you stay healthy and functional longer as you age. Participants in one study who spent time outdoors every day at age seventy had fewer complaints of aching bones, sleep problems, and other health-related problems at age seventy-seven than those who did not head outside every day. Being outdoors walking, gardening, or doing other hobbies increases mobility and decreases stress.[10]

Hike for Health

My grandmother walked to the market, and my mom biked. Me? I drive with my big minivan! But actually, I don't even have to leave the comfort of home to shop. Clothes, shoes, books, groceries, and much more can be ordered and delivered with the click of the mouse and a credit card number. As a society, we are moving less and sitting more. Our screens help us get work done, entertain us, teach us, and even help us get dinner on the table. But there are numerous health risks to being plugged in besides the uniquely twenty-first-century diseases of obesity, heart disease, and diabetes.

Consider your eyes. Spending the day in front of a screen can bring on headaches, burning eyes, or blurry vision. One way to alleviate eyestrain is to follow the 20–20–20 rule. Every twenty minutes, stare at an object twenty feet away for twenty seconds. This exercise for your eyes gives them a break from your giant monitor or tiny screen.[11]

Myopia (nearsightedness) is dramatically on the rise. In the United States, the rate of nearsightedness in people ages twelve to fifty-four increased by nearly two-thirds between the 1970s and early 2000s. It's much more pronounced in several Asian countries where 80 percent of 4,798 Beijing teenagers tested as nearsighted. In one study in Seoul, almost all the 24,000 teenage males surveyed were near-sighted.[12] Why the uptick? Apparently everyone, every-where, is spending too much time focusing on screens a few inches away and too little time watching for shooting stars at night or birds in the trees during the day.

Ears are in trouble too! People may joke about "Generation Deaf," but earbud-induced hearing loss is far too prevalent. Listening to music for just fifteen minutes at a hundred decibels can damage hearing. James often tells our kids emphatically, "You never get that hearing back!" As a reference, normal conversation is about 60 decibels, a lawn mower is 90 decibels, and a loud rock concert is about 120 decibels. If you can't hear anything going on around you when listening to earbuds, the sound level is too high. Lifelong hearing loss is increasing among teens at alarm-ing rates with the World Health Organization estimating 1.1 billion young people at risk. One in five teenagers have some form of hearing loss, a rate about 30 percent higher than in the 1980s and 1990s.[13] For using headphones, you can apply the 60/60 rule: keep the volume on the MP3 player under 60 percent and only listen for a maximum of sixty minutes a day.[14]

I can't imagine carrying around my eight-year-old

several hours per day. But that's what doctors say bending down to stare at your phone is like for your body. As your neck bends down to look at your phone, the weight on the spine increases. If your neck is tilted sixty degrees, it puts sixty pounds of pressure on your spine. "Text neck" is becoming commonplace as phone users spend an average of two to four hours per day hunched over, reading emails, sending texts, and scrolling through social media. That translates into 700 to 1,400 hours per year that people are putting stress on their spines.[15] Doctors compare the effects to bending a finger all the way back and holding it there for about an hour. Ouch!

Practice keeping your spine straight and relaxed, while directing your eyes toward your device rather than bending your neck. It's a natural tendency to hunch over the phone, but we can fight that tendency by sitting up straight and moving our heads left and right several times a day. Our necks, spines, and backs will thank us!

When I send a text, I either use the voice feature to talk into my phone, or I tap at it with my pointer finger. My thumbs are toast, probably from years of typing and lifting up babies. The thumb, however, is the digit of choice for most people while texting. Designed by God to grasp, hold, pinch, and grip, the thumb is now called upon to text, type, and swipe. Awkward angles and overuse can cause tendonitis or inflammation. If your thumbs ache or throb, take a "thumb break" along with your coffee break. Put your devices down frequently (think, "Hot potato") and give your thumbs regular times of rest.

You Don't Need a Tablet to Have Fun

Which activities do you enjoy? Let this list spark your imagination for something to get you up and out!

Archery

Baseball

Basketball

Beach Volleyball

Biking

Fishing

Flag Football

Gardening

Golfing

Hiking

Jogging

Jump Rope
Kayaking
Ping Pong
Rock Climbing
Rollerblading
Running
Sailing
Skateboarding
Skiing
Surfing
Swimming
Tennis
Ultimate Frisbee
Walking

Hit the Road

In chapter 1, I referenced the stories of grandparents who walked barefoot in the snow for miles to school uphill both ways. You might say today's child experiences the extreme opposite—they get dropped off at the shortest possible distance from the front doors and get picked up there too.

James remembers how healthy it was for him as a growing boy to ride his bike for miles and miles after school. He not only blew off adolescent steam, he gained confidence while learning how to make decisions independent of his parents.

Now that same day two of them were going to a village called Emmaus, about seven miles from Jerusalem. They were talking with each other about everything that had happened. As they talked and discussed these things with each other, Jesus himself came up and walked along with them. LUKE 24:13–15

Many modern parents are wary of such freedoms and worry about stranger danger or traffic accidents. I had such fears as my son began riding his bicycle to his new middle school. James was great, riding the three miles each way with Ethan for a few weeks, making sure Ethan knew the alternate routes and how to act at crowded intersections. We live in a suburb of San Diego, and Ethan attends a middle school of 1,800 students. James didn't let Ethan ride solo until Ethan had proven he knew how to handle stoplights, move with traffic, and pay attention to what was going on around him. I've had to bite my tongue on more than one occasion when I've wanted to worry out loud about the commute.

It takes a lot of parental discipline to "Take a Hike" and stop hovering over our children, checking in constantly with them through our devices. Our unhealthy over-involvement is producing unsure twentysomethings who don't know how to make basic decisions without checking in with Mom or Dad.

In the evening when I ask Ethan what his highlight from the day was, eight out of ten times he replies, "Biking." Getting outside and doing something physically challeng-ing gives him space to think, unwind, have fun, and grow strong. Parents, bless your kids by encouraging them to "Take a Hike" and get outdoors. Teach them the rules of the road when biking so they'll become more proficient drivers. It's easier to navigate through life when you know how to find your way home by yourself.

As we pull away from our devices and head outside more, even for five minutes, we'll be happier and healthier. Trips can be big (a vacation to a national park) or small (let's walk to the corner and back). Just keep moving. When you take that hike outdoors, leave your phone behind or tucked safely away in your pocket, never to see the light of day.

CREATING CALM

Take advantage of going outside at least once a day. Examine your daily routines and see where you can fit in a short walk or time to be outside.

TODAY'S PRAYER

Dear God, You have gloriously created the heavens and the earth. Forgive me for missing the splendor and silent witness of creation in my busy life. Open my eyes so I can see the divine order and beauty around me. May I consider the stars and how You call them each by name. May Your name be praised in all the earth. Thank You for making this beautiful world. In Jesus' name, amen.

Conclusion
Enjoy the View

He brought me out into a spacious place;
he rescued me because he delighted in me.

PSALM 18:19

When my kids were all in elementary school, we took a road trip from San Diego to Sedona, Arizona. We hiked the trails through the richly colored red rocks, looked up at the mountain formations, and searched for a famous rock that resembles Snoopy. I snapped a photograph at the Sedona airport overlook of my girls soaking in the majestic landscape. Did it take effort to get to that amazing spot? Yes, it took months of saving up money and hours in a minivan, but the views were totally worth it.

In a similar way, it will take effort for you to put down your phone when you crave checking your social media feed. Your friends may not be very happy when you don't text back within thirty seconds. You might get behind on a few television episodes. But trust me, those sacrifices will open a whole new vista, a wider space to enjoy. The view is up to you.

In that photograph of my girls at the Sedona overlook, Lucy is wearing a hoodie that looks like a panda. It's been years since she could fit into that old favorite. Noelle's looking through a telescope, wearing sandals that her younger sister wears now. How time has flown! I don't want to miss being present with my family because I was too busy experiencing life through a phone. Whether you're on vacation or walking up the same old walkway to your office, the view is up to you. What will you choose to notice?

When Lucy was two, we were trying to keep her quiet during Thanksgiving service at church—*very* quiet actually, as we were sitting right in front of the former senior pastor and his wife.

"Hi, Mommy!" she said to me.

She turned to James. "Hi, Daddy!"

"Hi Nana!" she said, turning to my mom. We gave her the harshest look we could muster and shushed her. A few minutes later, she stared at my face very intently then said in her normal volume toddler voice, "I like-a-your-face."

That I could not shush. James and I started laughing, so that it was us who needed shushing during the service. In focusing so intently on my face, Lucy was practicing the principle: *people first, phones second.*

I Am Not a Lab Rat

In his *Wall Street Journal* article "Take Back Your Brain from Social Media," Geoffrey Fowler wrote that "mindlessly checking Facebook makes you an awful lot like a lab rat habitually pressing a lever hoping for a pellet . . . but you're no rat. Human brains can resist the ways apps hijack our brains, if we learn a few coping skills."[1]

I certainly don't want my quality of life to be compared to a lab rat's! I want much more than screen-time pellets, and I know you do too. I don't want to be stuck in the same information-overload maze, day after day, waiting for the next hit. You and I are human, created in the image of God, and we can certainly choose to practice self-control with our devices. After doing what may seem hard at first, new digital habits will form in the days and weeks ahead.

The Bible instructs us many times to examine our ways and test them (Lam. 3:40; 2 Cor. 13:5; Gal. 6:4). We must be honest in evaluating how our digital life is impacting us spiritually and in our closest relationships. As we near the end of our *Calm, Cool, and Connected* book journey together, you're just beginning on a brand-new path of freedom. You've been deleting and decluttering your digital life, along with me. I hope we've become more *calm* in the storm, more *cool* under pressure, more *connected* to God and in our most important relationships.

New habits will soon run on autopilot. Keep practicing these five skills to move you to a better, more joy-filled space and peace:

H = Hold Down the Off Button

Have regular times in the day when you are powered off or away from your phone. Read your Bible or pray instead of checking your phone first thing in the day or last thing at night.

A = Always Put People First

Pivot away from your phone or computer when someone approaches you or starts a conversation. Make it your regular practice to look into the eyes of others and look up to God.

B = Brush Daily: Live with a Clean Conscience

As you brush your teeth each night, ask yourself, "Do I have a clean conscience before God? Have I wasted time online, watched evil, posted unkindly, or neglected others?"

I = I Will Go Online with Purpose

Before touching your phone or turning on your computer, ask the key question "What am I here to do?" Trade mind-numbing multitasking for laser-sharp focus and purpose.

T = Take a Hike

Go outside at least once a day. Schedule times to be outdoors without your eyes on your phone. Parents, remember to get your children outside sans screens too.

You may wonder if practicing these simple five habits daily will really change much. Wouldn't it be more emphatic and dramatic to go cold turkey and turn in our phones to a warden for, say, a month? Surprisingly experts don't recommend a complete digital detox. Instead, they suggest developing skills to manage social media and screen time as part of your everyday life.[2]

English writer Samuel Johnson (1709–1784) said, "The chains of habit are too weak to be felt until they are too strong to be broken."[3] That's true of bad habits, but it's also true of good ones. We can build strong new habits.

You may not instantly feel a difference when you pivot away from your phone to look into your child's eyes or when you take a quick break outside instead of scrolling through social media at your desk. But small changes pave the way for bigger changes. Small wins (you got through lunch without touching your phone) lead to big wins (you're talking to your teenager again).

A More Beautiful Path

You don't have to ditch your phone, tablet, or computer to live a calm, cool, and connected life. You just have to treat your devices differently. Don't approach your phone casually or you will casually check it All. The. Time. Now that you are more informed, you can picture a big yellow and black caution label over your screens. Use phones, TVs, and tablets with discretion to avoid overconsumption. Small steps are valuable ones. Just like Mary Poppins sang in the movie years ago, just a spoonful of sugar helps the medicine go down—a spoonful, not cups and cups of it.

You've heard those drug commercials that end with the announcer speaking at a rate ten times as fast: "Side effects may include nervousness, agitation, anxiety, insomnia, stomach pain, loss of appetite, nausea, vomiting, headache, vision problems, increased heart rate, numbness or tingling."

Slow that down. Those side effects sound awfully familiar, don't they? If you are like the average American, consuming more than ten hours a day of screen time, you've probably experienced some nervousness, agitation, and insomnia. You can leave behind those screen-time side effects. You're going to live differently. It will be well with your phone. You will not feel enslaved by texts, posts, or endless information anymore.

Your new calm digital lifestyle won't be perfect. Some days, you'll have a project at work that demands more screen time. Other times, you'll forget to look into your child's eyes because you're texting. When a setback happens, roll your shoulders back, take a deep breath, and begin again. The trick is making small corrections along the way. Practicing the five digital HABITs will keep you moving toward a more beautiful way of living.

Psalm 18:19 speaks of how God delivered David from

his enemies into a spacious place. God can do the same for you. You are not meant to get stuck halfway up the mountain, living a mediocre life. The enemy of your soul would love to keep you chasing notifications, posting comments, and using the bulk of your free time for entertainment. Technology can certainly be used to advance the kingdom of God, but many times it simply eats up our time.

Notice the personal pronouns David uses in Psalm 18:20–22: "The LORD has dealt with *me* according to *my* righteousness; according to the cleanness of *my* hands he has rewarded *me*. For *I* have kept the ways of the LORD; *I* am not guilty of turning from *my* God. All his laws are before *me*; *I* have not turned away from his decrees" (emphasis mine).

Like David, you can live righteously in an ungodly age. You can retire your phone from guiding your life and directing your steps. No matter what the world says, a fully charged phone in your pocket with Wi-Fi available can't provide what you need for a calm, cool, and connected life. Only God can give you that. As you walk humbly with God, He will bring you to a peaceful place, leading you to green pastures that restore your soul. Look up to God, not down to your phone, and enjoy the view.

Discussion Group Questions

Introduction: It Is Well with My Phone

1. Do you remember life before smartphones? What relational advantages and disadvantages did people have before smartphones?
2. Could you honestly say, "It is well with my phone," or would you like to see some improvement in this area?
3. Do you think devoting ten hours a day to screen time leads to a mediocre life? Why or why not?
4. What do you most want to get out of reading *Calm, Cool, and Connected*? Where do you think you need help?

Chapter One: Hold Down the Off Button

1. Do you have a hard time turning off your phone for meals, activities, church, dates, etc.?
2. Let's be honest. Do you need a digital pacifier? (See the "Do I Need a Digital Pacifier?" questions on p. 40–41.)
3. Parents, are you overly tethered to your children through technology? (Hint: if you're texting your child regularly at school, the answer is yes.)

4. Where is your phone when you sleep?

5. What is one calm, positive habit you will practice with your phone this week?

Chapter Two: Always Put People First

1. How are you doing giving eye contact to your loved ones, friends, and coworkers? Do people feel like they have your undivided attention when they are talking with you?

2. What are three scenarios in your daily life where you can practice The Pivot?

3. Does your spouse ever feel as if he or she is competing with a screen for your attention? Or vice versa?

4. The chapter ended with these words: *Your phone can't force you to use it. The video game can't make you play. The tablet can't even power on without your permission. Take control of your devices and make the commitment to put the people in your life first.* What devices do you need to get under control?

Chapter Three: Brush Daily: Live with a Clean Conscience

1. Have you ever been upset by something posted about you? What does that teach you about courtesy online?

2. There are many ways being online can get dangerous: pornography, video gaming, emotional affairs, seeking validation on social media, political rants, or shopping too much. Which of these are your particular temptations to watch out for?

3. Have you practiced asking yourself as you brush your teeth in the evening, "Have I brushed my heart? Do I have a clean conscience before God?"

4. How can you use technology to notice others and reach out to them in love?

Chapter Four: I Will Go Online with Purpose

1. How do you commonly waste time with technology? Here are few ways to get you thinking: texting, checking email, headline chasing, video games, TV, clicking on ads, cat videos.

2. How many minutes per day do you think you waste with screen time?

3. Have you asked, "What am I here to do?" before engaging with your devices? How has that helped you to focus? Or how could it help you?

4. What are your best productivity boosters you can share with others?

Chapter Five: Take a Hike

1. Talk about one of your favorite outdoor vacations. How do you feel when you are looking at something beautiful in creation?
2. Do you feel calmer and closer to God when you are outdoors in a peaceful, scenic environment?
3. Think about an average week. How much time do you spend outdoors? When you are outdoors, how much time do you spend looking down at your phone?
4. How could you get outdoors more often? What are a few activities you enjoy doing outside?

Conclusion: Enjoy the View

1. Which of the five habits struck a nerve with you?

   H = Hold Down the Off Button

   A = Always Put People First

   B = Brush Daily: Live with a Clean Conscience

   I = I Will Go Online with Purpose

   T = Take a Hike

2. What changes have you made with your technology since beginning this study?

3. How do you think your relationship with God can be affected by your phone, TV, tablet, computer, etc.?

4. How are you calmer, cooler under pressure, and more connected to God and others now?

10 Easy Questions to Connect

Can you name a favorite food of everyone around the table?

Where would you like to go on your next vacation?

Did you do anything nice for someone today?

What's your best fake foreign accent? Let's hear it.

What's your most prized possession?

What's one of your favorite movies?

How do you feel about social media? How do think it affects your relationship with others?

What's your definition of success?

What are you looking forward to at work or school?

What would you like to become better at?

Notes

Introduction

1. Technology Device Ownership: 2015, Pew Research Center, October 29, 2015, http://www.pewinternet.org/2015/10/29/technology-device-ownership-2015/.
2. *Merriam-Webster's Collegiate Dictionary*, 11th ed. (Springfield, MA: Merriam-Webster, 2003), also available at http://www.merriam-webster.com/.
3. Jacqueline Howard, "Americans devote more than 10 hours a day to screen time, and growing," CNN Health, July 29, 2016, http://www.cnn.com/2016/06/30/health/americans-screen-time-nielsen/.
4. David T. Neal, Wendy Wood, and Jeffrey M. Quinn, "Habits—A Repeat Performance," *Current Directions in Psychological Science* 15, no. 4. (Association for Psychological Science, Duke University, 2006), http://web.archive.org/web/20110526144503/http://dornsife.usc.edu/wendywood/research/documents/Neal.Wood.Quinn.2006.pdf.
5. Pastor Jeff Brawner, "The Responsibility Habit," sermon, Bonita Valley Community Church, Bonita, CA, July 17, 2016, http://bonitavalley.com/3437-2/.
6. Daniel Pink, "The Power of Habits—and the Power to Change Them," Daniel Pink blog, March 2012, http://www.danpink.com/2012/03/the-power-of-habits-and-the-power-to-change-them/.
7. Philip Yancey, "Guilt Good and Bad: The Early Warning Signs," *Christianity Today*, November 18, 2002, http://www.christianitytoday.com/ct/2002/november18/36.112.html.

Chapter 1: H = Hold Down the Off Button

1. L. Bernardi, C. Porta, P. Sleight, "Cardiovascular, cerebrovascular, and respiratory changes induced by different types of music in musicians and non-musicians: the importance of silence," *Heart*, 2006; 92(4):445–52, doi:10.1136/hrt.2005.064600.
2. Dr. Gary Chapman, personal interview, August 14, 2013.
3. Claire Groden / Fortune, "Here's How Many Americans Sleep with Their Smartphones," *Time*, June 29, 2015, http://time.com/3940023/sleep-banks-smartphones/.

4. Olga Khazan, "How Smartphones Hurt Sleep," *The Atlantic,* February 24, 2015, http://www.theatlantic.com/health/archive/2015/02/how-smartphones-are-ruining-our-sleep/385792/.

5. Margaret Heffernan, "The Truth About Sleep & Productivity," *Inc.,* January 26, 2012, http://www.inc.com/margaret-heffernan/the-truth-about-sleep-and-productivity.html.

6. "Are You a Nomophobe?" Iowa State University News Service, August 26, 2015, http://www.news.iastate.edu/news/2015/08/26/nomophobia.

7. "In Constant Digital Contact, We Feel 'Alone Together,'" interview with author Sherry Turkle, Fresh Air, *NPR,* October 17, 2012, http://www.npr.org/2012/10/18/163098594/in-constant-digital-contact-we-feel-alone-together.

8. David Andreatta, "As pay phones vanish, so does lifeline for many," *USA Today,* December 17, 2013, http://www.usatoday.com/story/news/nation/2013/12/17/pay-phone-decline/4049599/.

9. Proverbs 1:20.

10. Ecclesiastes 3:1–8.

11. Os Guinness, BrainyQuote, http://www.brainyquote.com/quotes/keywords/addiction.html#0Ffk1VP93VJ3qZbc.99.

Chapter 2: A = Always Put People First

1. Brian Alexander, "Put Down That Cellphone! Study Finds Parents Distracted by Devices," *NBC News,* March 10, 2014, http://www.nbc news.com/health/parenting/put-down-cellphone-study-finds-parents-distracted-devices-n47431.

2. Health enews staff, "Kids resent parents who are glued to their phones, study finds," *health enews,* Advocate Health Care, September 29, 2015, http://www.ahchealthenews.com/2015/09/29/kids-resent-parents-who-are-glued-to-their-phones/.

3. Psalm 123:1–2.

4. Lisa Eadicicco, "Americans Check Their Phones 8 Billion Times a Day," *Time,* December 15, 2015, http://time.com/4147614/smartphone-usage-us-2015/.

5. Joe Hadfield, "Too much texting can disconnect couples, research finds," *BYU News,* Brigham Young University, October 29, 2013, https://news.byu.edu/news/too-much-texting-can-disconnect-couples-research-finds.

6. *Merriam-Webster's Collegiate Dictionary,* 11th ed. (Springfield, MA: Merriam-Webster, 2003), also available at http://www.merriam-webster.com/.

7. Eadicicco, "Americans Check Their Phones 8 Billion Times a Day."

8. Anne Fishel, "The most important thing you can do with your kids? Eat dinner with them." *The Washington Post,* January 12, 2015, https://www.washingtonpost.com/posteverything/wp/2015/01/12/the-most-important-thing-you-can-do-with-your-kids-eat-dinner-with-them/.
9. Napoleon Hill, quoted at BrainyQuote, http://www.brainyquote.com/quotes/quotes/n/napoleonhi393807.html.
10. Jayson Demers, "How Much Time Do Your Employees Waste at Work Each Day?" *Inc.,* August 20, 2014, http://www.inc.com/jayson-demers/how-much-time-do-your-employees-waste-at-work-each-day.html.

Chapter 3: B = Brush Daily: Live with a Clean Conscience

1. "Cyberbullying/Bullying Statistics," *Statistic Brain,* date of research February 19, 2016, http://www.statisticbrain.com/cyber-bullying-statistics/.
2. Danica Lo, "Survey Says: Social Media Sets Unrealistic Beauty Standards," *Glamour,* February 19, 2015, http://www.glamour.com/story/social-media-self-esteem.
3. Adrian Rogers, "The Poison of Pornography," *oneplace,* May 13, 2014, http://www.oneplace.com/ministries/love-worth-finding/read/articles/the-poison-of-pornography-15292.html.
4. Ron DeHaas, "What are the most up-to-date stats on pornography?" *Covenant Eyes,* January 19, 2016, http://www.covenanteyes.com/2016/01/19/what-are-the-most-up-to-date-stats-on-pornography/#.
5. Victor B. Cline, "Pornography's Effects on Adults & Children," 2002, *Scribd,* https://www.scribd.com/doc/20282510/Dr-Victor-Cline-Pornography-s-Effects-on-Adults-and-Children.
6. Lynn Marie Cherry, "Why We Will Be Using Covenant Eyes for Life," *Covenant Eyes,* October 20, 2016, http://www.covenanteyes.com/2016/10/20/why-we-will-be-using-covenant-eyes-for-life/.
7. Marilynn Wei, MD, JD, "10 Signs You're Addicted to Online Shopping," *Psychology Today,* November 4, 2015, https://www.psychologytoday.com/blog/urbansurvival/201511/10-signs-you-re-addicted-online-shopping.
8. Jason O. Gilbert, "'Selfie,' 'Tweep,' and 'Hashtag' Added to Merriam-Webster Dictionary," Yahoo! Tech, May 19, 2014, https://www.yahoo.com/tech/selfie-tweep-and-hashtag-added-to-86215489849.html.
9. John Ortberg, *The Me I Want to Be: Becoming God's Best Version of You* (Grand Rapids, MI: Zondervan, 2010), 187.
10. Lauren F. Friedman "13 Awful Things That Happen If You Don't Brush and Floss Your Teeth," *Business Insider,* February 14, 2014, http://www.businessinsider.com/what-happens-if-you-dont-brush-and-floss-your-teeth-2014-2.

Chapter 4: I = I Will Go Online with Purpose

1. Cat Zakrzewski, "The Key to Getting Workers to Stop Wasting Time On-line," *Wall Street Journal,* March 13, 2016, http://www.wsj.com/articles/the-key-to-getting-workers-to-stop-wasting-time-online-1457921545.
2. Joshua Leatherman, "How to Use Batching to Become More Productive," Michael Hyatt blog, July 8, 2011, https://michaelhyatt.com/how-to-use-batching-to-become-more-productive.html.
3. Molly Brown, "Survey shows that average U.S. worker spends 6.3 hours checking email every day," *Geek Wire,* August 26, 2015, http://www.geekwire.com/2015/survey-shows-that-average-u-s-worker-spends-6-3-hours-checking-email-every-day/.
4. Laura Vanderkam, "Stop Checking Your Email, Now," *Fortune,* October 8, 2012, http://fortune.com/2012/10/08/stop-checking-your-email-now/.
5. "What Is the Pomodoro Technique?" Cirillo Company, n.d., http://cirillocompany.de/pages/pomodoro-technique/.
6. David Russell Schilling, "Knowledge Doubling Every 12 Months, Soon to Be Every 12 Hours," *Industry Tap,* April 19, 2013, http://www.industrytap.com/knowledge-doubling-every-12-months-soon-to-be-every-12-hours/3950.
7. Mark Milian, "Study: Multitasking hinders youth social skills," CNN, September 12, 2016, http://www.cnn.com/2012/01/25/tech/social-media/multitasking-kids/.
8. Stephanie Vozza, "What Happened When I Gave Up Social Media for a Month," *Fast Company,* July 6, 2016, https://www.fastcompany.com/3061454/your-most-productive-self/what-happened-when-i-gave-up-social-media-for-a-month.
9. "The Myth of Multitasking," Talk of the Nation, *NPR,* May 10, 2013, http://www.npr.org/2013/05/10/182861382/the-myth-of-multitasking.
10. Peter Bregnman, "How (and Why) to Stop Multitasking," *Harvard Business Review,* May 20, 2010, https://hbr.org/2010/05/how-and-why-to-stop-multitaski.html.
11. Ibid.
12. Bob Sullivan and Hugh Thompson, "Brain, Interrupted," Sunday Review, *New York Times,* May 3, 2013, http://www.nytimes.com/2013/05/05/opinion/sunday/a-focus-on-distraction.html?_r=0 .
13. Chris Woolston, M.S., "Multitasking and Stress," HealthDay, January 20, 2017, https://consumer.healthday.com/encyclopedia/emotional-health-17/emotional-disorder-news-228/multitasking-and-stress-646052.html.

Chapter 5: T = Take a Hike

1. Damien Carrington, "Three-quarters of UK children spend less time outdoors than prison inmates—survey," *The Guardian,* March 25, 2016, https://www.theguardian.com/environment/2016/mar/25/three-quarters-of-uk-children-spend-less-time-outdoors-than-prison-inmates-survey.
2. Neil E. Klepeis, et al., "The National Human Activity Pattern Survey (NHAPS): a resource for assessing exposure to environmental pollutants," *Journal of Exposure Science & Environmental Epidemiology* (2001) 11, 231–52. 10.1038/sj.jea.7500165, http://www.nature.com/jes/journal/v11/n3/full/7500165a.html.
3. Robin Mejia, "Green exercise may be good for your head," *Environmental Science & Technology,* 2010, 44(10), 3649. 10.1021/es101129n, http://pubs.acs.org/doi/full/10.1021/es101129n.
4. Dr. Gary Chapman, personal interview, August 14, 2013.
5. Dr. Sanjay Gupta, "The Light Stuff: 4 Ways to Brighten Life," *Everyday Health,* May 23, 2014, http://www.everydayhealth.com/news/light-stuff-ways-to-brighten-life/.
6. Harvard Medical School, "A prescription for a better life: go alfresco," *Harvard Health Publications,* July 2010, http://www.health.harvard.edu/newsletters/Harvard_Health_Letter/2010/July/a-prescription-for-better-health-go-alfresco.
7. Laurie F. Friedman, and Kevin Loria, "This Might Be the Easiest Way to Boost Concentration and Memory," *Business Insider,* August 10, 2014, http://www.businessinsider.com/boost-concentration-and-memory-by-going-outside-2014-8.
8. Abigail Wise, "Here's Proof Going Outside Makes You Healthier," *Huffington Post,* June 22, 2014, http://www.huffingtonpost.com/2014/06/22/how-the-outdoors-make-you_n_5508964.html.
9. Harvard Medical School, "A prescription for a better life: go alfresco."
10. J. M. Jacobs, et al., "Going Outdoors Daily Predicts Long-Term Functional and Health Benefits Among Ambulatory Older People," *Aging Health,* April 2008 20(3):25–72. 10.1177/0898264308315427, https://www.ncbi.nlm.nih.gov/pubmed/18332184.
11. Sharon Profis, "Five surefire ways to reduce computer eyestrain," *Cnet,* June 1, 2012, https://www.cnet.com/how-to/five-surefire-ways-to-reduce-computer-eyestrain/.
12. Shirley S. Wang, "The Puzzling Rise in Nearsighted Children," *Wall Street Journal,* April 20, 2015, http://www.wsj.com/articles/the-mysterious-spike-in-nearsighted-children-1429543997.

13. "Generation Deaf: Millennials and Earbud-Induced Hearing Loss,"/ *Florida Hospital*, June 8, 2016, https://www.floridahospital.com/blog/ generation-deaf-millennials-and-earbud-induced-hearing-loss.

14. Susan Donaldson James, and Kathryn Nathanson, "Generation Deaf: Doctors Warn of Dangers of Ear Buds," *NBC News*, June 8, 2015, http:// www.nbcnews.com/health/health-news/generation-deaf-doctors-warn-dangers-ear-buds-n360041.

15. Lindsey Bever, "'Text neck' is becoming an 'epidemic' and could wreck your spine," *Washington Post*, November 20, 2014, https://www .washingtonpost.com/news/morning-mix/wp/2014/11/20/text-neck-is-becoming-an-epidemic-and-could-wreck-your-spine/?utm_term= .bde64efc2916.

Conclusion: Enjoy the View

1. Geoffrey A. Fowler, "Take Back Your Brain from Social Media," *Wall Street Journal*, February 1, 2017, https://www.wsj.com/articles/take-back-your-brain-from-social-media-1485968678?mod=ST1.

2. Ibid.

3. Samuel Johnson, quoted at BrainyQuote, https://www.brainyquote.com/ quotes/authors/s/samuel_johnson.html.

About the Author

Arlene Pellicane is a speaker and the author of several books including *31 Days to Becoming a Happy Mom* and *Growing Up Social: Raising Relational Kids in a Screen-Driven World* (coauthored with Gary Chapman). She has been featured on the *Today Show, Fox and Friends, Focus on the Family*, and *Family Life Today*. She lives in San Diego with her husband, James, and their three children. Find out more at ArlenePellicane.com.

What kids need to know in a screen-driven world

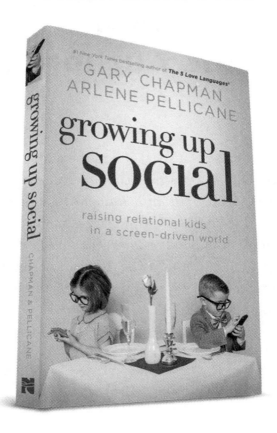

Children today are spending more and more time interacting with a screen, and less time with a parent. In *Growing Up Social*, you'll discover the five skills needed to give your child relational success in a screen-driven world, helping them value what matters most.

978-0-8024-1123-5 │ also available as an eBook

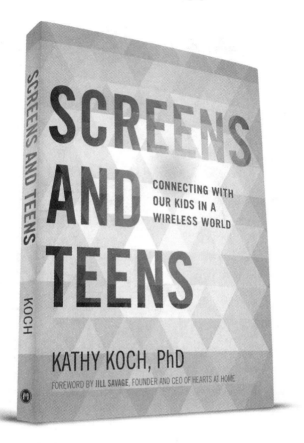

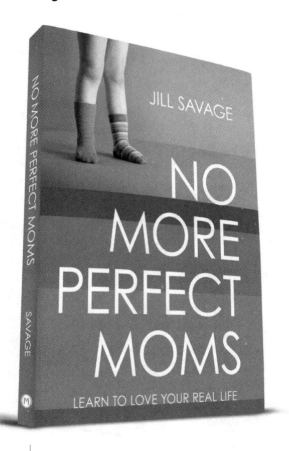